Contents

Introduction

Researchers in psychology, linguistics, sociology and education have added enormously to our understanding of how we all learn to become readers. Reading is a complex process: we need to draw on a whole range of cueing strategies in our search to make meaning of print.

For instance, we use:

▲ prior knowledge of what happens and how people behave, think and feel, in real life and in books

▲ context – the meaning of the surrounding text

▲ syntax – knowledge of how the grammar of the English language works

▲ grapho-phonic information – recognizing whole words instantly; understanding the relationship between letters and sounds; using spelling patterns to make analogies with known words.

Children need a great deal of practice in all these strategies before they can use them automatically to make sense of print quickly and accurately. The aim of all primary school teachers is to enable children to do just that – to use all strategies in concert by processing in parallel their knowledge of the world, of books, of grammar, of letters, sounds, word patterns and the developing meaning of the text.

But there is more. It is a paramount responsibility for all teachers to help children to become critical readers who can discriminate between the shallow and the multi-layered, who can read between and beyond the lines, and use their inferential skills to respond to the deeper meanings of texts. Such readers respond wholeheartedly to the emotional impact of a text; they consider the range of attitudes conveyed by particular characters; they understand how different points of view are conveyed by the author; they perceive the underlying issues in a text. It is every child's entitlement to feast on books that get them thinking in this way.

The demands made on readers have increased dramatically over the years. Children nowadays come face to face with print in a variety of forms. In this book we address four main areas, namely, print in the environment, poetry, narrative and non-fiction. Each of these four sections begins with a brief, focused introduction highlighting the key points for consideration within that sphere.

The Literacy Hour

The aim of this book is to support teachers in their efforts to provide interesting activities to stimulate children's development in all of these areas. In this book we follow the systematic approach within a set structure advocated by the National Literacy Strategy, that is, we begin with the whole class working together, followed by group or pair work, with a final whole class session for reflection on the key learning points. We indicate in each case whether the key learning point(s) fulfil requirements for work at text, sentence and/or word level. Text level involves comprehension and composition of whole texts; sentence level concentrates on grammar and punctuation; word level incorporates the teaching of phonics, spelling and vocabulary development. We offer opportunities for a range of focused discussions about texts, as well as close observation of sentence construction, individual words and, of course, reading aloud with expression. Recent studies support earlier findings that sound–symbol associations are most readily consolidated when children are engaged in writing, thus activities for reading and writing are integrated throughout this book.

Also, young children learn more easily when the task is purposeful in their eyes, otherwise they tire easily and can become disillusioned or bored. Try, therefore, to avoid decontextualized exercises and aim for activities that grow naturally from engagement with the meaning of the text. In all sessions, it is important to remember that whatever the focused teaching point, enjoyment and involvement with the meaning of the book remain top priority. Books should be shared for their own sake in the first instance, not because they are useful for teaching specific skills. We must guard against using books in classrooms in any way that detracts from their intrinsic value. Focused work should always enhance enjoyment, and interest in language.

When the practical suggestions within this book draw on specific texts, we suggest a small number of key narrative, poetry and non-fiction books, which are readily available and popular with children. However, the general ideas can be applied to any worthwhile book, sentence-level suggestions to any grammatical construction, and the phonic approaches to any combination of sounds or spelling patterns that occur in English.

Lesson plans

The structure for each activity is as follows:
Detailed lesson plans, under clear headings, are given for each activity and provide material for immediate implementation in the classroom. The structure for each activity is as follows.

Activity title box

The box at the beginning of each activity outlines the following key aspects:

▲ *Learning objective.* The learning objectives break down aspects of the programmes of study for English into manageable teaching and learning chunks. They can easily be referenced to the National Curriculum for England and Wales and the Scottish National Guidelines 5–14 by using the overview grid on pages 7–12.

▲ *Class organization/Likely duration.* The icons **††** and ⊕ indicate the suggested group sizes for each activity and the approximate amount of time required to complete it.

Previous skills/knowledge needed

This section gives information when it is necessary for the children to have acquired specific knowledge or skills prior to carrying out the activity.

Key background information

This section outlines the areas of study covered by each activity and gives a general background to the particular topic or theme, outlining the basic skills that will be developed and the way in which the activity will address the children's learning.

Preparation

Advice is given when it is necessary for the teacher to prime the pupils for the activity, to prepare materials or to set up a display or activity ahead of time.

Resources needed

All materials needed to carry out the activity, including photocopiable pages, are listed here.

What to do

Clear step-by-step instructions are provided for carrying out the activity. These include (where appropriate) suitable questions for the teacher to ask the children in order to help instigate discussion and stimulate a high quality of writing.

Suggestion(s) for extension/support

In these sections, ways of providing differentiation are suggested.

Assessment opportunities

Where appropriate, opportunities for ongoing teacher assessment of the children's work during or after the activity are highlighted.

Opportunities for IT

Where relevant IT work would strengthen an activity, appropriate possibilities are outlined.

Display ideas

Where they are relevant and innovative, display ideas are incorporated into the activity plans, perhaps illustrated with examples.

Other aspects of the English PoS covered

Inevitably, as all areas of English are interrelated, activities will cover aspects of the programmes of study in other areas of the English curriculum. These links are highlighted under this heading.

Reference to photocopiable sheets

Photocopiable activity sheets are provided for use with particular activities. Small reproductions of these are included in the appropriate lesson plans, together with notes on their use and (where appropriate) suggested answers to questions.

Overview Grid

This grid helps you to track the coverage of the Reading part of the Programme of Study for English at Key Stage 1, or the Scottish National Guidelines for English Language 5–14 at Levels A–B, offered by the activities in this book. For each activity, the relevant statements from the National Curriculum for England and Wales and the Scottish 5–14 Guidelines are indicated (the latter references are given in italics).

Most of the activities in this book are linked to the *Curriculum Bank* for Reading at Key Stage 1/Scottish Levels A–B. These links are indicated by footnotes below the relevant activities. The grid also shows how the activities relate to the Key Objectives set out in the Literacy Framework.

ACTIVITY TITLE	LEARNING OBJECTIVE	POS/AO	NLS	CONTENT	PAGE
Signs all around	To explore different ways of representing information, including print. To recognize and understand signs and symbols in the environment. To read on sight common words from everyday situations in isolation. To recognize critical features of words.	2b. *Reading for Information: Level A.*	R WL5, TL1	Exploring signs and symbols in the environment. Whole-class work and working in pairs.	13
We're going on a print hunt, page 14					
Weather reports	To recognize signs and symbols connected with a specific topic. To read on sight common words from everyday situations.	2b. *As above.*	R WL5	Looking at vocabulary and symbols associated with weather reports. Whole-class work and working in pairs.	15
Beneath the surface, page 18					
Shops: What's in a name?	To read on sight a range of familiar words. To arrange in alphabetical order a collection of familiar words. To be aware of the use of capital letters for proper nouns. To generate families of rhyming words.	2a. *As above.*	R SL4, WL1; Y1 T1 TL12, 14	Exploring features of shop names and developing an understanding of rhyme and alphabetical order. Whole-class and groups work; groups reporting to rest of class.	17
T-shirt bazaar, page 16					
Doing the shopping	To increase their vocabulary of words recognized on sight. To consolidate their understanding of the relationship between print and sound symbols. To read on sight familiar words on labels.	2b. *As above.*	R WL5, 11; Y1 T1 WL8	Looking at signs and notices and writing lists. Whole-class and group work.	19
Food fair, page 22					
Breakfast cereals	To pay increasing attention to the significant features of words. To become critically aware of language used to persuade. To read information presented in a variety of forms.	1b. *Reading for Information: Level B.*	Y1 T1 WL10, TL13	Looking at information presented by manufacturers and answering questions about it. Whole-class and group work.	21
Food fair, page 22					
Inn signs	To build their vocabulary of words recognized instantly. To further develop their interest in words. To read aloud their own stories with expression to a large group.	2b, c. *Reading Aloud - Imaginative Writing: Level B.*	Y1 T1 WL8, 12, TL13	Writing stories and developing the ability to read aloud to an audience. Whole-class brainstorming exercise; work as individuals and as groups.	23
We're going on a print hunt, page 14					

ACTIVITY TITLE	LEARNING OBJECTIVE	POS/AO	NLS	CONTENT	PAGE
Tickets please!	To become confident in interpreting print in all its forms. To be aware of the design features that support a reader.	1b, d. *Reading for Information: Level B.*	Y1 T1 TL12	Investigating the information found on tickets and working in pairs to design tickets. Whole-class and group work.	24
We're going on a print hunt, page 14					
A car boot sale	To increase the vocabulary of words they can read instantly. To develop awareness of different styles of writing for different purposes.	1b; 2d. *Functional Writing: Level B.*	Y2 T1 SL5, TL18	Exploring and designing advertisements for events. Whole-class and pairs work.	25
Estate agents' advertisements, page 28					
Similarities and differences	To describe story settings and incidents and relate them to their own experiences. To identify and discuss characters' appearances, personalities, behaviour.	1c; 2c. *Reflecting on the writer's ideas and craft: Level B.*	Y1 T2 TL7–9	Listening to a story and exploring it in relation to real life situations. Whole-class and pairs work.	28
Expressing fears, page 62					
Who's talking?	To identify speech marks in reading, understand their purposes and use terms correctly. To investigate and recognize ways of presenting text (speech bubbles and so on).	2a; 3. *Knowledge about Language: Level B.*	Y2 T2 SL6	Exploring the use of speech marks and developing their use. Whole-class and group work.	30
Creating a class comic, page 40					
Alliteration	To consolidate the discrimination of initial phonemes. To identify alliteration in known words.	1c; 2b. *Reading for Enjoyment: Level B.*	Y2 T2 WL4, TL9	Children writing their own alliterative sentences after studying alliteration. Whole-class and group work.	32
Playing with language, page 87					
Text completion	To predict story endings, such as unfinished extracts. To read aloud their finished stories to the class.	1c; 2c. *Reflecting on the writer's ideas and craft: Level B.*	Y1 T3 TL14; Y2 T2 TL13	Writing endings for a story which has been read to the class. Whole-class and group writing work and reading aloud.	33
Babysitters, page 50					
Complex sentences	To be more aware of the grammatical structures, namely relative clauses. To generate complex sentences using relative clauses, modelled on the text.	1d; 2b. *Knowledge about Language: Level B.*	Y2 T3 SL5	Working in groups reading and writing complex sentences.	34
Holidays, page 58					
Opposites	To explore antonyms. To collect and discuss differences in meaning.	2b; 3. *As above.*	Y2 T2 WL11	Exploring antonyms related to the weather and matching opposites. Whole-class work, then individual, pairs and groups work.	36
Television advertisements, page 32					
Real and imagined lives	To discuss familiar story themes, linked to their own experiences.	1d; 2c. *Responding to the writer's ideas and craft: Level B.*	Y2 T1 TL6; Y2 T2 TL7	Preparing a dramatic retelling of a story. Whole-class work, then small groups for presentations.	37
Pets, page 54					

(Left vertical label for section: NARRATIVE)

ACTIVITY TITLE	LEARNING OBJECTIVE	POS/AO	NLS	CONTENT	PAGE
Narrative structure	To develop knowledge of narrative structure. To learn terms such as 'narrative', 'character', 'setting', 'plot'.	1a, c, d; 2c; 3. *Knowledge about Language: Level B.*	Y2 T1 TL4; Y2 T2 TL5	Whole-class and paired work exploring story structure.	39
Traditional tales, page 64					
Short story genre	To explore the similarities and differences between two literary genres, novels and short stories.	1c, d; 3. *Awareness of Genre: Level B.*	Y2 T3 TL5, 7	Group work analysing differences between two literary genres.	41
African folk tales, page 68					
Listen and learn	To listen carefully to a poem being read aloud. To learn by heart and recite a poem with predictable and repeated sound patterns. To recognize and experiment with a repetitive rhythmical pattern.	1c; 2b, c. *Reading for Level B.*	R WL1, TL10; Y1 T2 TL11	Listening to, discussing and then completing poems with repetitive rhythmical patterns. Whole-class and group work.	43
Games, rhymes and songs, page 74					
Keep listening and learning	To extend their knowledge of types of poetry. To enjoy poetry containing patterned language. To recognize and experiment with sound patterns and rhyme. To read and learn a humorous animal poem.	1c; 2b, c. *As above.*	R WL1, TL10; Y1 T2 TL11	Whole class listening to and learning a poem.	45
Rhyming stories, page 80					
Listen, learn and think!	To extend rhyming patterns by analogy, generating new words. To discriminate onsets and rimes.	1c; 2b. *As above.*	R WL4; Y1 T1 WL6, TL6	Whole class listening to pems and studying rhyme. Groups finding rhyming words.	47
Nursery rhymes, page 77					
Creating a class anthology	To extend their experience of poetry by collecting favourite poems for a class anthology. To identify and discuss favourite poems and poets, using appropriate terms - poet, poem, verse, rhyme, rhythm. To recognize when reading aloud is effective. To participate in reading poems aloud. To show good presentational skills when reading aloud.	1a, c, d. *As above.*	Y1 T3 WL10, TL11; Y2 T1 TL8; Y2 T2 TL11	Individual and paired work exporing poetry and creating a class anthology.	49
Poems, page 92 (especially page 94); Cloze procedure, page 99					
Critics' corner	To discuss poems read. To compare and contrast themes in poems. To comment on patterns of sound, word combinations and forms of presentation. To discuss meanings of words and phrases that create humour and sound effects in poetry.	2a, b. *Responding to the writer's ideas and craft: Level B.*	Y1 T3 TL10; Y2 T2 TL11	Whole class, followed by pairs or individuals, commenting critically on poetry.	51
Nursery rhymes, page 77					
Poetry festival	To be introduced to poems by significant children's authors. To be introduced to poems from a range of cultures. To practise reading aloud to an audience.	1d; 2c; 3. *As above.*	Y2 T2 TL11	Whole class studying a range of poetry.	52
Poems, page 92					

ACTIVITY TITLE	LEARNING OBJECTIVE	POS/AO	NLS	CONTENT	PAGE
All join in!	To learn and recite a new poem. To extend a poem following the rhythm of the original. To discriminate syllables in words. To develop phonological awareness and identify initial sounds.	1d; 2a. *Reading for Enjoyment: Level A.*	Y1 T2 WL1, TL11; Y2 T2 WL5, TL9	Whole class and pairs exploring various features of poetry.	53
Poems, page 92					
Visiting poet	To become well-acquainted with the work of one poet. To read a range of different text types with confidence.	1d. *Responding to the writer's ideas and craft: Level B.*	Y1 T3 TL9; Y2 T3 TL6	Exploring the work of one poet and preparing for the poet's visit.	55
Poems, page 92 (especially page 95)					
Anything they can do...	To use humorous verse as a structure to write their own poems by adaptation, mimicry or substitution.	1d; 2b, c. *Imaginative Writing: Level B.*	Y2 T2 TL15; Y2 T3 TL8, 11	Writing humourous verse based upon the structure of an established poem.	57
Nursery rhymes, page 77 (especially page 79); Playing with language, page 89					
Listen and write	To select words with care, re-reading and listening for effect. To use similes and alternative words and phrases to express meaning.	2b, c. *As above.*	Y2 T2 SL3, TL15	Individual and whole-class composition of poems after listening to music.	59
Playing with language, page 89 (especially pages 88–89)					
Look and write	To look closely. To make inferences and predictions. To further develop their understanding of poetic form. To read their poems in a familiar setting. To prepare and present poems to a larger audience.	2b, c. *As above.*	Y2 T2 TL15	Writing poems individually or in pairs or small groups after looking at paintings.	61
Children's playground games, page 84					
Memories are made of this	To select words with care, re-reading and listening for effect. To discuss these effects within a familiar group. To read own work with expression to a familiar audience.	1a; 3. *As above.*	Y2 T1 TL9, 12	Whole-class poetry writing about treasured possessions.	63
African folk tales, page 68 (especially page 70)					
My family	To use speech bubbles correctly. To write from personal experience. To prepare and present poems to a familiar audience.	1a; 2b; 3. *Personal Writing: Level B.*	Y2 T2 SL6–7	Whole-class and individual poetry writing on the theme of families.	64
Pets, page 54					
Pet phrases	To engage in a shared reading and writing activity to create a co-operative class poem. To prepare and present poems based on familiar settings.	1a; 2b; 3. *Reading Aloud: Level B.*	Y2 T2 TL11; Y2 T3 TL6	Whole-class reading and writing of poetry.	66
Animal tales, page 71					

	ACTIVITY TITLE	LEARNING OBJECTIVE	POS/AO	NLS	CONTENT	PAGE
NON-FICTION	Naming parts	To use all available cueing strategies to recognize words in isolation. To note similarities and differences between words. To match labels to the correct body part. To practise Look/Say/Cover/Write/Check routines for learning words. To read and use labels with confidence and build sight vocabulary on a specific topic.	2a, b. *Reading for Information: Level A.*	R WL2, 5, 9; Y1 T1 WL10; Y1 T2 WL7	Whole-class and group work on the vocabulary of parts of the body.	68
	Food fair, page 22					
	What can we do with our bodies?	To read labels and captions competently on a specific topic. To read information presented in the form of a Venn diagram. To understand the function of verbs. To be aware of the number of syllables in words. To use strategies for finding information quickly.	2a, b, d. *As above.*	Y2 T2 WL5, SL5, TL18–19	Whole-class and paired work focusing upon the verbs related to parts of the body.	70
	Toys and games, page 115					
	Keeping fit	To formulate and read aloud questions on a specific topic. To explore different ways of representing information. To interpret meaning from graphs and charts.	1b; 2d. *Functional Writing: Level B.*	Y2 T3 SL6, TL14, 21	Whole-class and pairs conducting a survey and presenting information.	72
	Seasonal weather, page 108					
	Illnesses and accidents	To scan a chart quickly in order to answer questions. To use pictures as an aid to scanning for information. To observe a picture carefully and infer meaning from the sub-text, going beyond the literal. To read their own writing aloud to the class.	1b; 2b. *Reading for Information: Level A.*	Y1 T3 TL19, 22	Whole-class and paired or individual work compiling charts and interpreting a picture.	75
	Seasonal weather, page 102					
	A healthy diet	To revisit dictionary skills. To identify simple questions and use structural guiders in a non-fiction text to locate information effectively. To use a key-word scanning card to find relevant information quickly. To identify the main points and gist of a text by noting or underlining. To evaluate information from a range of sources. To recognize that non-fiction books on similar themes can give different information. To practise scanning charts to retrieve information quickly.	1b; 2b. *As above.*	Y1 T3 TL17, 19; Y2 T2 TL16–17, 21	Whole class, pairs and individuals working for three sessions: finding information, answering questions and completing and interpreting charts.	77
	Evaluating information books, page 102					

ACTIVITY TITLE	LEARNING OBJECTIVE	POS/AO	NLS	CONTENT	PAGE
Keeping our bodies comfortable	To develop confidence and competence in using the Dewey system or school colour-coded system to locate books. To develop information retrieval skills, using structural features of non-fiction texts. To skim-read a book in order to find out what it is about. To read reflectively to take on board new knowledge and remember it.	1b; 2a, d. *Reading for Information: Level B.*	Y2 T3 TL15–17	Paired work investigating clothing, using reference sources.	81
Evaluating information books, page 102					
Wood	To develop awareness of linguistic features that support comprehension. To develop skills for reading aloud to large groups. To further develop research strategies.	1b; 2a, d. *As above.*	Y1 T2 TL18, 25; Y2 T3 TL15–16	Individual, group and whole-classs research into wood.	83
Growth, page 104					
A walk in the woods	To develop independent research skills, by using a simple writing frame. To use the structural guiders in a non-fiction book to locate information quickly. To write a non-fiction book, providing structural guiders for readers.	1b; 2a, d. *As above.*	Y2 T1 SL6, TL15	Whole-class and group work preparing for a visit and gathering and presenting information.	85
Growth, page 104					
From trees to tables	To use a range of cueing strategies to read an unknown text. To reorder a text in a logical sequence. To scan books for relevant information on a given topic. To be aware of the characteristics of process writing.	1b; 2b, d. *As above.*	Y2 T2 TL19, 21	Individual or paired exploration and production of ordered texts.	87
Making an information book, page 120					
Paper	To read and carry out a set of instructions. To know that it is essential when describing a process to sequence the steps correctly. To further develop research skills. To read their own writing to the class.	1b; 2a, d. *As above.*	Y1 T3 TL19; Y2 T1 TL13–14	Reading and using instructions. Devising and answering questions using reference sources.	89
Making books, page 112					
Fire	To make explicit what they already know about a specific topic, and generate questions about what they need to find out. To use structural guides to scan texts and find relevant information quickly. To recognize that non-fiction books on similar themes can give different information and present similar information in different ways. To compare information from a range of sources.	1b; 2a, d. *As above.*	Y1 T3 TL17–22; Y2 T3 TL13–17, 19	Groups using a range of reference sources and developing an understanding of non-fiction texts.	91
Evaluating text books, page 102					

Print in the environment

This chapter provides a selection of activities related to the print that surrounds children in their everyday lives – the words, signs and symbols they see on the street, in shops, on television, in the junk mail that pours through their letter boxes. Here we build on their innate curiosity about the world around them, the words they see repeatedly and learn to associate with meaning – words that inform, warn, prohibit, persuade. These activities will help children to look carefully and to hold images in their minds by focusing on significant features of words, such as shape, length, initial letters, spelling patterns, words within words. They will therefore help to extend children's sight vocabulary, a crucial factor in learning to read with confidence, fluency and accuracy. But, perhaps most importantly of all, by starting with words that children already know from their immediate surroundings, these activities will help children to develop the skill of reading new words by making analogies with the ones they know.

They will also encourage children to note how writers play with language in order to attract the attention of readers and persuade them to respond in a certain way.

These activities provide a range of ideas for fulfilling the requirements of the Literacy Hour, especially at text and word levels.

SIGNS ALL AROUND

For the children to: explore different ways of representing information, including print; recognize and understand signs and symbols in the environment; read on sight common words from everyday situations in isolation; recognize critical features of words.

✝✝ *Introductory oral session: whole class. Children working on their own or in pairs. Feedback session: whole class.*

🕐 *Introductory oral session: 20 minutes. Individual/ pair work session: 15–20 minutes. Feedback session: 15–20 minutes.*

Previous skills/knowledge needed

It would be helpful if children are aware that meaning can be represented in a variety of forms, and have some experience of 'reading' pictures, signs and symbols as well as words.

Key background information

Technological advances have meant that we are bombarded with a mass of information in an ever-increasing variety of forms – newspapers, magazines, teletext, notices, slogans, diagrams, charts, maps, illustrations, photographs, collages, videos, signs, symbols, logos, and so on – as well as continuous printed text in books. Children now have to be able to interpret many different vocabularies in order to function effectively in today's society.

This activity begins this process by promoting close observation of signs and symbols that occur close to home, in any and every neighbourhood. It could be used for Literacy Hour work at word level.

Preparation

Collect photographs, books and/or illustrations of a range of everyday public signs that the children are likely to be familiar with such as Parking, Telephone, Cycle Lane, Hospital, Toilets, No Dogs, No Smoking, No Right Turn, No Left Turn, No Parking, Bus Stop. Choose a selection that includes both words and symbols, if possible.

Resources needed

Examples of signs and symbols, a copy of photocopiable sheet 94 for each child, scissors and glue, a flip chart or board.

What to do

Show the class your collection of signs and symbols and ask the children if they have seen them in the local area or elsewhere, perhaps when visiting relatives and friends, or when on holiday. Talk about where exactly they saw them, and what they think they are telling us. Discuss whether they are all easily understood, whether there is any ambiguity or risk of misunderstanding, whether symbols are easier to read than words, whether the writing style, colours chosen, size, and so on make for easy visibility. Ask the children what suggestions they have for improving clarity and instant understanding. You might like to tell them the story of the little girl from Australia who thought the No Right Turn sign meant that you could not throw boomerangs!

Focusing on one or two word signs, recap together the features to look for so you can hold a mental picture of a word in your head, such as initial letter, word length, spelling patterns, syllables.

Hand out copies of photocopiable sheet 94 and explain to the children that they can work on their own or in pairs to complete the activity by putting the signs in the correct places on the street scene.

When they have finished, share results, and recap on factors that help instant word recognition, such as initial letters, length and shape of words, spelling patterns.

Round off the session with a quick words-within-words game to support children's observational skills and visual memory, for example 'Hospital' = a/it/pit/spit.

Suggestion(s) for extension

To extend their range, ask some children to make a note of all the signs they see on their way to school – maybe a road sign, bus stop sign, shop name, street name, notice in a shop window, and so on. You could then provide the children with a simplified map of the local area and ask them to make a set of appropriate sign cards to stick on it. They could make this into a board game with a set of instructions for younger children to play. They could practise these words with the Look, Say, Cover, Write, Check routine with a friend in order to consolidate reading and spelling skills.

Suggestion(s) for support

Where necessary, you could support children's word recognition, when working with the photocopiable sheet, by continuously drawing their attention to key features in the words and by making helpful comments, such as 'I think you know this word – it's on that sign just outside our school.'

To consolidate word recognition children could:
▲ play Pelmanism, snap and/or Kim's game with a set of word cards
▲ play lotto and dominoes with a set of matching word and symbol cards
▲ be given a set of the words discussed, with some letters missing for them to provide
▲ find words that rhyme with the given words

▲ find words that have the same spelling pattern as the given words
▲ find words that all begin with a particular letter
▲ sort out a set of signs wrongly placed on a street photo.

Assessment opportunities

Note children's skills of instant word recognition, of interpreting symbols, of remembering features that help us to recall words.

Opportunities for IT

You could use IT to make enlarged signs for the display.

Most reading packages have software programmes to support initial letter discrimination and develop sound–symbol relationships, which would benefit some children.

Display ideas

You could use 'recycled' food cartons and boxes to mount a 3-D display of a local street with shops and houses, roads and pavements, zebra crossings, and so on, complete with signs in words and symbols.

Other aspects of the English PoS covered

Speaking and listening – 1c; 2a, b.
Writing – 2d.

Reference to photocopiable sheet

Photocopiable sheet 94 asks that children interpret the picture and symbols and read the signs correctly in order to place them in appropriate positions.

WEATHER REPORTS

For the children to: recognize signs and symbols connected with a specific topic; read on sight common words from everyday situations.

†† *Oral sessions: whole class. Introductory session: whole class. Children working in pairs.*

⏲ *Oral sessions: 5 minutes each. Introductory session: 15 minutes. Pair work session: 20–25 minutes.*

Previous skills/knowledge needed

It would be helpful if children were already familiar with vocabulary associated with the weather, such as: rain, sunshine, snow, hail, sleet, fog, mist, gale, flood.

Key background information

This activity continues the process of learning to read everyday signs and symbols, in this case related to a particular topic, the weather, and draws on children's interest in different media. It requires children to interpret symbols and to use a range of cueing strategies to complete a cloze procedure text. It could be used in the Literacy Hour to develop work at word and sentence level.

Preparation

Ask the children to watch television weather reports at home and to note the vocabulary and the symbols used. Encourage them to look at weather reports in the family newspaper too. Make an enlarged (A3) copy of a newspaper weather report to look at with the whole class, and an enlarged map of the British Isles for the class weather chart. Make detachable symbols for the chart.

Resources needed

Card and materials for making detachable symbols for the class weather chart, a map of Britain, writing and drawing materials, copies of photocopiable page 95 for children to work in pairs.

What to do

Each morning, ask the children to tell you about the television weather forecast of the previous evening including temperature and wind factors, and then to describe the prevailing weather conditions in your area at the present time.

Gather the class together to consolidate their learning. You could comment on the symbols used on television to illustrate the weather types, such as blobs for rain, fluffy cloud shapes, rays for sun, arrows for wind direction, numbers for wind speed and for temperature. You could discuss the blue and red lines for the hot and cold fronts moving across the country. Ask the children if they noticed any words as well as symbols, such as 'weekend weather', a day of the week, 'today', 'tonight', 'low', 'high', 'windy', 'mostly dry', 'mild', 'cloudy', 'outbreaks of rain'. Talk about any warnings that the reporter gave, such as cold weather warnings for old people, icy roads for motorists.

Then focus on the enlarged weather report from the daily newspaper, looking closely at the words and symbols, such as 'Around Britain', 'the world', 'air quality', 'sun and moon', 'lighting-up', 'high tides'. Discuss the significance of all these categories of information: *Who needs to know about tides? Why is it important to know lighting-up time? What use is knowledge of air quality?* Read the words together from around the map of Britain – windy, moderate, slight, rough, fog – and talk about their meanings. Find your local area on the map to check your forecast for the day.

Towards the end of the week, when the children have become familiar with the vocabulary and symbols, organize them into pairs and hand out copies of the photocopiable sheet 95. Explain to them that they have to look closely at the weather map and translate the symbols into words to fill the gaps in the weather report.

Suggestion(s) for extension

To help learn spelling patterns, children could hunt for words like 'high' that have the pattern *-igh* in them; they could also collect adjectives like 'windy' that end in *-y*

Provide regular opportunities for children to learn new words with a partner using the LSCWC routine.

Suggestion(s) for support

In the whole-class situation, teachers need to gauge their questions carefully to ensure that all children can respond successfully when asked.

Word-within-word games will help to reinforce word recognition for those children with an immature visual memory.

To develop understanding of sound–symbol relationships, children could list words beginning with the same blends as weather words, for instance snow and sleet.

Assessment opportunities

Note children's reading strategies when working from the weather report, and their ability to interpret symbols and to read information from a map.

Opportunities for IT

Children could compile a dictionary of weather words in alphabetical order.

Display ideas

Display the large weather map of the British Isles. Stick appropriate symbols on each day and call upon individual children to make the necessary changes each day.

A frieze depicting all the rhymes concerned with weather would be an attractive classroom backdrop.

The class could also collect stories, poems and songs with weather as a theme or in the title, and read or recite them together during the week. For instance: 'Doctor Foster', 'Rain rain go away', 'I hear thunder', 'One fine day', 'The house that sailed away', 'Aio the rainmaker', 'The day the tide went out and out and out'.

Other aspects of the English PoS covered

Speaking and listening – 1a, c; 2a, b; 3a.
Writing – 1c; 2a.

Reference to photocopiable sheet

Photocopiable sheet 95 requires children to interpret the symbols on a map of Britain in order to complete the accompanying descriptive text.

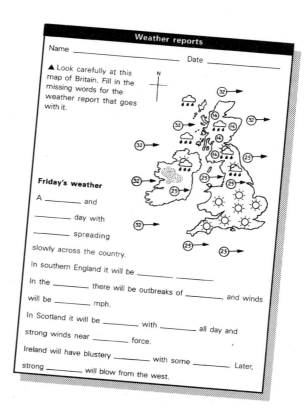

SHOPS: WHAT'S IN A NAME?

For the children to: read on sight a range of familiar words; arrange in alphabetical order a collection of familiar words; be aware of the use of capital letters for proper nouns; generate families of rhyming words.

†† *Writing session: children working in small groups. Oral sessions: groups report to whole class. Children working alone. Final session: whole class.*

🕐 *Writing session: 35 minutes: Oral sessions: 15 minutes each. Individual work session: 10 minutes. Final session: 10–15 minutes.*

Previous skills/knowledge needed
It would be helpful, but not essential, that children have a growing awareness of the critical features in recognizing words, such as length, shape, initial letters, spelling patterns, words within words.

Key background information
Children's understanding of sound–symbol relationships and phonological awareness needs to keep expanding, alongside a growing understanding of the importance of the visual aspects of words. It is crucial to keep building sight vocabulary in order to secure reading progress.

You will need to ensure that all the names of shops that feature on the photocopiable sheet have been mentioned in the whole-class session.

Here, the focus is on work at word level.

Preparation
Ask the children to note in their jotters over a couple of weeks the names of all the shops in the area – from their immediate vicinity and the nearest town centre, national chains and local firms, across the full range of goods and services.

Resources needed
Large sheets of paper, writing materials, a flip chart or board, access to a computer, a copy of photocopiable sheet 96 for each child.

What to do
Divide the children into small groups and give each group a couple of large sheets of paper. You could encourage one group to work directly on the computer. Give each group a specific target, such as a particular type of shop – supermarket, department store, clothes shop, bank, record, electrical, DIY, hairdresser, bookstore, and so on.

Ask them to write on their large sheet of paper or computer screen all the shops from their lists in their jotters that fall into their given category. Remind them to use a capital letter for a shop name. Then tell them to put them in alphabetical order.

When the task has been completed, the groups in turn can share their findings with the whole class. Sharing results would be best organized by group in short sessions, rather than trying to fit all the groups into one very long session. You could add a few names of your own, perhaps from visits to other parts of the country or from TV advertising, and write them on the flip chart. As you look at the lists, focus on ways of helping the children to recognize words on sight. Then, have a quick quiz game: *Can you tell me the names of three shops that begin with the same letter; two shops that rhyme with…; four shops with two/three/four syllables in their names; a shop with the little word 'at' in its name?*

Hand out photocopiable sheet 96 for the children to complete in order to consolidate their learning. They are asked to read the rows of shop names, circle the odd one out in each case, and then give a reason.

Finally, discuss with the whole class the reasons behind the shop names. For instance:
▲ the original owner's family name – Marks and Spencer, Burton, Boots, Sainsbury, Blackwell
▲ an indication of what's on sale inside – The Body Shop, Homebase, Iceland
▲ a suggestion of good value for money – Our Price, Kwiksave
▲ a hint of the good quality and freshness of the products on sale – Top Shop, Safeway.

Suggestion(s) for extension
Children could collect words that rhyme with shop names, for instance with Monsoon – boon, balloon, cartoon, harpoon, maroon, moon, noon, pantaloon, platoon, Rangoon, saloon, soon, spoon.

Suggestion(s) for support
Mixed ability grouping for the written tasks will provide support for less experienced readers and writers. It would also boost confidence to ensure that they have a task within the group team that they will be able to accomplish successfully, for instance ticking off names rather than writing alphabetical lists.

Assessment opportunities
Monitor children's growing competence in reading names in isolation, their ease in categorizing shops and ordering alphabetically, their use of capital letters to write shop names, and their ability to recognize and generate rhyming words.

Opportunities for IT
Alphabetical lists could be compiled using IT, as could all the items for the display. Some children would benefit from working with the Oxford Reading Tree software, *Rhyme and Analogy*, which is available on disk or CD ROM, and/or *Pattern and Rhyme* in the 'Talking Stories' package from Ginn's *All Aboard* series.

Display ideas
Each group could choose a shop and list what it sells, the price range it caters for, the extra services it offers, the appeal of the shop layout, and so on, within the outline of its building.

Other aspects of the English PoS covered
Speaking and listening – 1a, c; 2a, b.
Writing – 1c; 2a, d, e; 3b.

Reference to photocopiable sheet
Photocopiable sheet 96 provides children with the opportunity to consolidate learning and to extend their vocabulary of words recognized on sight. They choose the odd one out amongst the shop names and give a reason for their choice.

Shops

Name _____ Date _____

▲ Read the shop names below and put a ring around the odd one out in each row. Then give your reason.

1 McDonald's, Mothercare, Wimpy, Burger King
Why? _____

2 Boots, TopShop, Burton, Etam
Why? _____

3 British Home Stores, Littlewoods, Woolworths, Dolcis
Why? _____

4 Asda, Tesco, Iceland, Safeway
Why? _____

5 Toys Я Us, Currys, Southern Electric, Dixons
Why? _____

6 Our Price, Barclays, HMV, Virgin
Why? _____

▲ Now make up some more for your friends to do:

DOING THE SHOPPING

For the children to: increase their vocabulary of words recognized on sight; consolidate their understanding of the relationship between print and sound symbols; read on sight familiar words on labels.

†† *Session One*: whole class. *Session Two*: Oral session: whole class. Writing session: group work. Feedback session: whole class.

🕐 *Session One*: 10 minutes. *Session Two*: Oral session:15 minutes. Writing session: 30 minutes. Feedback session: 15–20 minutes.

Previous skills/knowledge needed

This activity will form part of an ongoing programme for developing children's phonological awareness and their sight vocabulary.

Key background information

It is imperative to awaken and extend children's interest in words by encouraging them to look around them when out and about for print used in their environment. Parental support for raising awareness in this way is most helpful, so forge links with home as quickly as possible. Looking closely at words and considering their sounds and spelling patterns should become an automatic habit for children.

Session Two is organized along the lines of the Literacy Hour and covers work at word level.

Preparation

It would be helpful to write to parents in advance to ensure their support in helping children to carry out the supermarket survey.

Resources needed

A flip chart or board, large sheets of paper, writing materials, copies of photocopiable sheets 97 and 98 for children needing support.

What to do

Session One

In a brief five-minute session, ask the children about their family's shopping habits. How often do they shop for food – daily, weekly, fortnightly, monthly? Do they usually do their main shopping at a supermarket or in small local stores? Who does the shopping – mum, mum and dad, mum and children, dad and children, the whole family? What do they like/dislike about going shopping? Ask if they have ever noticed any signs in the shops and scribe on the flip chart or board what they remember. Suggest that they accompany their parent(s) on their next food-shopping trip and make a note of all the signs they see to share in class the following week.

Session Two

With the whole class gathered together, write on the flip chart the signs the children have seen on their shopping trips. You could work randomly, or begin by finding out which shops they went to and, starting with the most popular one, take them in turn in order to compare similarities and differences between them.

Divide the class into groups, perhaps according to which supermarket they visited, and ask them to sort the sign-names into sets. (More than one group session may be needed, according to the children's experience and ability.) Decide together what sets you might consider. For instance:

▲ main sections of the store (Fruit and Vegetables; Butcher's Counter; Fresh Fish; Beers, Wines and Spirits; Bakery; Delicatessen; Dairy; Groceries)

▲ type of product on offer in the various aisles (such as Pasta, Rice, Oils, Sauces, Cakes, Biscuits, Home Laundry, Pet Food, Home Baking, Kitchenware, Jam and Preserves, Tea and Coffee, Crisps and Snacks, Breakfast Cereals, Frozen Pies, Chips, Ice Cream, Cheese, Yoghurt)

▲ specific products available there (such as, in the Fresh Meat aisle: Beef, Pork, Lamb, Chicken, Turkey, Steaks and Joints, Casserole and Stewing, Sausages and Burgers)

▲ extra information for customers (in the bakery section: Bread as fresh as it gets; Our bread is always freshly baked; Our skilled bakers bake each loaf with care and pride)

▲ drawing attention to prices (Special Offer; Low price; 20% off for one week only; Buy 2 get 1 free; Reduced to clear; Unbeatable Offers; Half Price)

▲ extra services (Customer Toilets; Customer Services; Suggestions Box; Coffee Shop; Newspapers and Magazines; National Lottery; Photo Service)

▲ warning signs (Staff Only; Out of order; Caution – Wet Floor; Cleaning in Progress; We apologize for any inconvenience caused to our customers; Fire Exit; No Smoking)

▲ notices outside the store (Parking area; Disabled; Mother and Toddler parking; Petrol; Recycling).

Allow the children about 30 minutes to work on their lists, then gather the class together to discuss their findings. Talk about variations in terminology, amount of information, range of products and services, how the stores had grouped them and so on. Discuss with the children how helpful the notices were for finding products quickly. Ask for their suggestions to improve visibility, accessibility, layout. Were there any major omissions? Why did they think products were grouped together as they were? Would they have organized things differently? Why?

Suggestion(s) for extension

More confident children could put their lists into alphabetical order, or underline in different colours recurring spelling patterns in their word lists, such as *ea*/*ee*/*ui*/*ou*.

The game 'Scoop' from H.E.L.P. Educational Games focuses on vowel digraphs, such as *ea*/*ai*/*ee*, and may be useful as a follow-up activity.

Suggestion(s) for support

Some children will require the support of an adult to help them read labels, sort them into alphabetical order and write out/word-process the list to present to the class. They would also benefit from re-sorting into appropriate categories jumbled sets of words, using photocopiable sheets 97 and 98.

Children needing extra support in word recognition could also:

▲ play matching lotto/domino/snap/Pelmanism games with words from their lists

▲ group words beginning with the same initial letter – baked beans, bread, biscuits, beer, beverages, burgers, beef, breakfast, butter, bacon

▲ group words with the same spelling pattern – st*ea*k, cl*ea*r, r*ea*dy, m*ea*t, unb*ea*table

▲ group words with the same number of syllables – pet, food, beans, snacks; baking, coffee, kitchen, stewing, toilets; sausages, casserole, beverages, customer

▲ generate further lists of words by working with onsets and rimes – m/*eat* – b/*eat* – bl/*eat* – ch/*eat* – f/*eat*, and so on.

Assessment opportunities

During discussions note children's awareness of the uses of categorization, their word recognition skills, their awareness of spelling patterns, their confidence and effectiveness when working as team members.

Opportunities for IT

Some groups could use a computer to compose their lists.

Display ideas

You could create a mini-supermarket in the classroom for role-play situations, with the children providing labels to help make it look authentic.

Other aspects of the English PoS covered

Speaking and listening – 1a, c; 2a, b; 3b.
Writing – 1a; 2d, e; 3b.

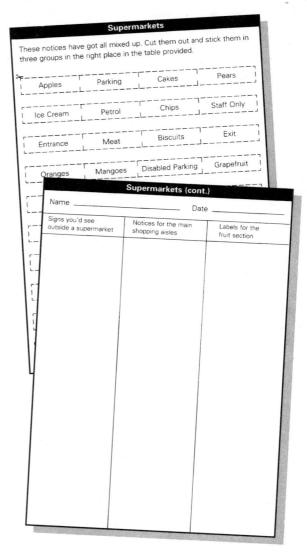

Reference to photocopiable sheets

Photocopiable sheets 97 and 98 can be used to help less experienced children to recognize words from everyday situations in isolation. They are required to re-sort jumbled lists of words according to given criteria.

BREAKFAST CEREALS

For the children to: pay increasing attention to the significant features of words; become critically aware of language used to persuade; read information presented in a variety of forms.

†† *Session One: whole class. Session Two: Oral session: whole class. Reading session: children working in small groups. Feedback session: whole class.*

🕐 *Session One: 15 minutes. Session Two: Oral session: 20–30 minutes. Group work session: 20–25 minutes. Feedback session:15–20 minutes.*

Previous skills/knowledge needed

This activity should be part of a programme to raise children's general language awareness. Ideally, children will already have carried out a shopping print survey (see 'Doing the shopping' on page 19).

Key background information

Children need to be made aware that language can be used to persuade readers, and that advertising is a prime example of this. Encourage them to read between the lines to interpret underlying meanings, and to pay particular attention to the 'small print' to be sure of the facts. This activity provides work at text, sentence and word levels.

Preparation

Seek parents' co-operation for the work to be undertaken during the family shopping trip. Encourage children to bring in empty cereal packets to be used during group work.

Resources needed

You will need sufficient cereal packets for the group investigations, a flip chart or board, writing materials, copies of photocopiable sheet 99 for the children designing their own cereal packets.

What to do

Session One

If the children have already carried out a shopping print survey, praise them for their successful survey of supermarket signs and tell them that they are now going to look more closely at one particular product, breakfast cereal.

Find out what they already know about cereals – be sensitive, as always, as some children may come to school without having had any breakfast at all, and some may eat cereal for tea or supper. Scribe on the flip chart the cereals that children in the class eat regularly, ones they would like to eat, ones they eat occasionally (perhaps for a treat) and the alternatives to cereals that some children might eat.

Ask the children to continue their supermarket searches this week by noting on their next shopping expedition all the different types of cereal on sale there, ready for a class discussion.

Session Two

Pool the information on cereals and write the names on the flip chart or board. You could arrange them randomly, in alphabetical order or in groups according to, say, the grain used. Talk to the class about which cereals are usually

eaten hot and which cold, whether they would add anything extra to them, such as sugar, chopped fruit, honey, cream. Which words have been specially chosen and why? Who do they think the names are intended to appeal to – old people, children, parents? What do the various names mean (such as muesli), and what do they think the difference is between flakes, crispies, crunchies, pops, puffs, Shreddies, wheaties, Frosties? What do they think is most important about cereals – the cost, the texture, the taste, health factors?

Divide the class into groups to hunt for information from the packets, such as all the named ingredients; amounts of sugar, protein and so on; which words tell us facts and which opinions. Are the facts clear? Which words have been specially chosen to attract customers? What sort of words are these usually?

When group work has been completed, share findings as a class and sum up. Highlight the use of persuasive language – the number of adjectives, the choice of adjectives (accuracy or exaggeration?), the type of sentences (long and complex or short and pithy?),the overall tone (sophisticated or chatty and jocular?), the use/ overuse of certain sorts of punctuation marks.

Suggestion(s) for extension

Some children could invent their own brand of cereal and use photocopiable sheet 99 to design packaging and write advertising blurb for it. Remind them of the features mentioned above – the short, snappy sentences used in most adverts, together with the use of expressive adjectives and of language features, such as alliteration, onomatopoeia, rhyme and a surfeit of exclamation marks.

Suggestion(s) for support

It may be advisable for you to work with a specific group to guide their thinking throughout by using more restricted prompt questions and comments, that is, closed questions or ones that demand making a choice between only two alternatives.

Children who need more practice of new words in isolation could collect words that particularly appeal to them from the various cereal packets, practise with the LSCWC routine and then make matching games for younger children to play.

Assessment opportunities

Monitor children's growing awareness of the significant features of words, their growing sight vocabulary and their understanding that language can be used to persuade.

Opportunities for IT

Children could use an IT Art programme to design their cereal packet.

Display idea

Create a gallery of collages made from cereal packets with a border of recipes interspersed with advertising slogans.

Other aspects of the English PoS covered

Speaking and listening – 1a, c; 2a, b; 3b.
Writing – 1c; 2a, c, d, e; 3b.

Reference to photocopiable sheet

Photocopiable sheet 99 provides children with the opportunity to design a cereal packet, invent a name for the cereal and write their own advertising slogan, putting into practice some of the points raised in the class discussion.

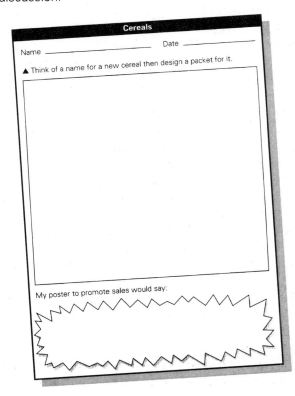

INN SIGNS

For the children to: build their vocabulary of words recognized instantly; further develop their interest in words; read aloud their own stories with expression to a large group.

✝✝ *Brainstorming session: whole class. Children working on their own or in pairs. Preparation sessions: individual work. Reading sessions: whole class.*

🕐 *Brainstorming session: 15 minutes. Individual/pair work sessions: 30 minutes each. Preparation sessions: 5 minutes each. Reading sessions: 10–15 minutes each.*

Previous knowledge/skills needed

It is assumed that children have some experience of writing narrative.

Key background information

Here is another chance to extend children's interest in words, their origins and meanings. Ongoing opportunities in meaningful contexts for developing children's library and research skills are an essential component of sound literacy teaching. Children need time to prepare for reading aloud with fluency and meaningful expression.

The initial focus of the activity is on word-level work, but it then shifts to sentence and text levels.

You may find it helpful to familiarize yourself with the topic by consulting *Pub Names of Britain* by Leslie Dunkling and Gordon Wright (Orion) and the *Wordsworth Dictionary of Pub Names* (Wordsworth).

Preparation

A display of photographs and books on inn signs and other street furniture would help to motivate the children.

Resources needed

A flip chart or board, paper or work books, writing materials.

What to do

Brainstorm with the children a list of names of inns and pubs that they have come across in the local neighbourhood, a nearby town, on visits to friends or relatives, on holiday, on television programmes, and in books they have read. You are likely to have a collection that includes names of animals such as The White Hart, The Rat and Parrot, The Fox and Hounds, The Red Lion, The Dog and Duck, The Dun Cow, The Pig and Whistle, The Black Swan; names of people such as The Queen's Head, The Turk's Head, The Marquis of Granby, The Duke of Wellington, The Rover's Return, and some that do not fit into either of those categories, such as The Barley Mow, The Wheatsheaf, The Beehive and The Tap and Spile.

Discuss with the children the meaning of any unusual words (dun, meaning a greyish brown) and the possible stories behind the names: *Does the Red Lion refer to a real lion? If so, why did it look red? How did it come to be in the United Kingdom? What happened to it? Why is the inn called after it? Or might it be the lion on a coat of arms? Did a famous knight fight a heroic battle here? Who won? Did he die a tragic death?*

Ask the children to work on their own or in pairs to choose an inn name, then plan and write the story behind the name, which they can then read aloud to the rest of the class. (The number of sessions required for this will vary according to the experience of the children.) Remind them of the features that captivate readers – a good beginning, logically sequenced events, interesting details, suspense, surprise, appeal to the emotions, a lively style with varied sentence structure, expressive vocabulary, asides to the reader, and so on. Remind them also of editing and proof-reading skills, such as checking spelling, grammar and punctuation.

Throughout the week, allow children time to prepare for reading aloud to the class. Talk through the factors that help to make reading aloud effective, such as pausing, stressing important words, changing the pace of the reading, changing the volume, using gestures and facial expression. Then, set up story-reading sessions when the children read their stories in turn. Encourage them to comment on each other's good reading aloud strategies.

Suggestion(s) for extension

Confident readers could be encouraged to make tape recordings of their reading for the listening corner. They could also present their project in a school assembly.

Some children could investigate in the library the origins and meanings of names – not only of inns, but of towns, families, first names and so on, or create their own inn name, design a sign for it, and then write the story of how it came about.

Suggestion(s) for support

Working in a small group, a pair or with an adult helper when writing their story or preparing their reading will give confidence to less experienced children.

Assessment opportunities

Note children's confidence in large group discussions, their accuracy when reading inn names from the flip chart, their delivery when reading their stories to the class or in assembly, and their planning, drafting and editing skills when writing their stories.

Opportunities for IT

The stories could be 'published', with the editing process done on the computer.

Display ideas

Mobiles of inn signs could be hung around the classroom. The children's stories could be 'published' in a class collection.

Other aspects of the English PoS covered

Speaking and listening – 1a, c; 2b; 3b.
Writing – 1a, b, c; 2b, c, d, e; 3b.

TICKETS PLEASE!

For the children to: become confident in interpreting print in all its forms; be aware of the design features that support a reader.

✠ *Writing session: small groups. Oral session: whole class. Children working in pairs.*

🕐 *Writing session: 20 minutes. Oral session: 30 minutes. Design session: 15–20 minutes.*

Previous skills/knowledge needed

It would be helpful if children were already used to noting how texts are presented, for example the use of enlarged print, bold, italics.

Key background information

Both as readers and writers, children need to become increasingly aware of the range of possibilities for presenting texts. A computer is an ideal tool for exploring these possibilities.

This activity could be used for Literacy Hour work at text level.

Preparation

Ask the children to keep any of their family's used tickets over a period of a couple of weeks and bring them into school. Make your own collection of tickets; they may add to the variety produced by the children.

Resources needed

Ticket collection, a flip chart or board, writing paper, writing and drawing materials for designing a ticket.

What to do

Divide the class into small groups of mixed ability to look at the selection of tickets they have collected and to make a list of all the information provided on the front of each one, such as place, event, date, time, price, seat number, and on the back of each one, perhaps a box office phone number, conditions of sale or advertisements.

When this task has been completed, gather as a whole class to pool findings. First of all, find out what sorts of tickets were involved and record the range on the flip chart.

Note the wide variety – add some of your own, if necessary, – such as transport (bus, train, underground, ferry, aeroplane); entertainment (cinema, pantomime, horse show, theatre, concert, fireworks, circus, puppet show, dance); sport (football match, ice rink, roller skating, swimming pool, gym, athletics meet); visits (zoo, museum, gallery, theme park); miscellaneous (cloakroom, parking).

Then discuss the need for a ticket, from the point of view of the seller and the buyer! *Who checks, and what might happen if you have not got one? What could you do if you lose one?*

Lastly, share the information the groups found on the tickets and discuss the usefulness of the information, durability of material, size and type of font, colour combinations, clarity, and so on. Using these criteria, the class could vote on the best design.

The children now work in pairs to design a ticket for a forthcoming event in school.

The class could carry out a similar investigation into junk mail. How much do they receive at home each week? What sorts of items are included – free newspapers, supermarket offers, flyers for fast-food deliveries, financial advice, estate agents' blurb, travel offers, food coupons? How much use are they? What happens to most of them? What can be done about it? What sort of language is used to try to persuade readers to buy, invest, donate?

Suggestion(s) for extension
Some children could rework a ticket to improve its design, then send their version to the place concerned, explaining their reasons for redesigning the ticket.

Suggestion(s) for support
Where unfamiliar vocabulary is involved, an adult helper could be assigned to the group to help read the information on their tickets by prompting them to use a range of cueing strategies.

Assessment opportunities
Note children's strategies when reading the information on the tickets, and their ability to apply design skills when making their own tickets.

Opportunities for IT
Lists and accounts of the survey for display could be produced using various formats on the computer.

Display ideas
The class could mount a factual display, giving a descriptive account of their ticket survey and listing their results or create a collage of the tickets they designed themselves.

Other aspects of the English PoS covered
Speaking and listening – 1a; 2b.
Writing – 1b; 2d, e.

A CAR BOOT SALE

For the children to: increase the vocabulary of words they can read instantly; develop awareness of different styles of writing for different purposes.

†† *Introductory session: whole class. Children working in pairs. Design session: pair work. Publishing sessions: whole class.*

🕐 *Introductory session: 10 minutes. Pair work session: 30 minutes. Design session: 40 minutes. Publishing sessions: 25–30 minutes each.*

Previous skills/knowledge needed
It would be helpful if children have experience of looking at the features of words that help them to hold a visual image in their mind, such as length, shape, initial letter, spelling patterns, words within words, syllables. Children with previous experience of alliteration and wordplay could draw on these features also. Some experience of 'publishing' their writing would be very helpful.

Key background information
This activity will help to broaden children's range of experiences with factual information, and will help to increase their accuracy of reading words in isolation. To maximize learning, it is preferable for literacy activities to be embedded in genuine situations rather than hypothetical ones, so it is hoped that a real car boot sale, or equivalent, can be organized in school.

This activity provides experience at text and word levels.

Preparation
Cut out and make enlarged photocopies of adverts for car boot sales from local papers, and collect out-of-date flyers from local shops and lamp-posts.

Resources needed

Examples of car boot sale adverts and flyers; art, writing and book-making materials; a flip chart or board.

What to do

Spend a few minutes with the whole class talking about car boot sales (or equivalent) that they have been to – where, when, goods on sale, goods they bought, the crowd of visitors, amusing incidents, and so on. Tell them that you are going to organize a car boot sale / jumble sale / flea market / collectors' fayre at school to support charity, and that there is a lot of work to be done to make sure it goes well.

Show them a selection of the flyers and newspaper advertisements that you have collected, and explain that they will have to design similar adverts in order to ensure a good turnout on the day to support the school's charity. Remind or tell the children of the sort of language that attracts readers' attention, and suggest that alliteration might come in useful here too to attract customers to their car boot sale.

Divide the children into pairs to scrutinize the adverts and list the information they will need to put on theirs. When they have finished, share ideas and decide on the 'essential items' to appear on their advert – place, date, starting time, ticket price, range of goods, directions to the school, the charity concerned, something special to attract customers – and write these on the flip chart as a reminder. Discuss other important features such as layout, spacing, print style and size, colours, handwriting, IT.

During the week the children can design their advertising flyers ready for distribution to the local shops.

Make sure photographs are taken at the event to serve as illustrations when the class 'publish' a book afterwards celebrating the event. After the sale, several sessions will be needed for the children to 'publish' the book.

Suggestion(s) for extension

Some children can produce the labels and price tickets for the goods on sale, as well as some larger notices to indicate toilets and so on, and others to encourage customers to buy.

Suggestion(s) for support

Mixed ability pairings for this activity will lend confidence to less experienced children, while for some, the support of an adult helper might be required. Thoughtful allocation of tasks when 'publishing' the book will ensure a successful outcome for all children.

Assessment opportunities

Note children's reading strategies as you circulate round the pairs, and also their attention to the details of the print. You can monitor their design skills when they make their flyers, and their planning, writing and editing skills when preparing the book.

Opportunities for IT

DTP packages are ideal for children to use to produce their flyers and to 'publish' their books.

Display ideas

You could have a 'work in progress' board before the event, showing all the jobs to be done and who has undertaken to do them: sketches for advertising flyers, a map of the playground or field for stall placement and car parking; labels and price tickets.

The book of the event, when completed, should take its rightful place in the school library.

Other aspects of the English PoS covered

Speaking and listening – 1a, c; 2a, b; 3b.
Writing – 1b, c; 2a, b, c, d, e; 3a.

Narrative

The reading environment

The quality of the books that children encounter, and of the discussions that ensue, goes a long way towards creating a nation of avid readers, but other classroom experiences have a part to play too. Books need to be kept in high focus, for instance, via assembly presentations, library visits, 'critics' corner', thematic displays, 'author of the week' celebrations, Book Week activities, lunchtime story club, school bookshop, workshops with visiting authors and illustrators.

Children need to be involved regularly in private reading, paired, shared and group reading, reading to adults, listening to taped stories and poems, re-enacting stories with puppets or props, and having stories read aloud to them at least once a day.

This puts books at the heart of learning to read where they belong, and provides some admirable starting points for the Literacy Hour for working at text, sentence and word level.

The importance of talk

Discussion is a key factor in the experience of reading. The importance of talking about books is well documented, so we must ensure that time is available after reading for children to respond spontaneously to what they have heard or read, and to reflect on the ideas encountered. Indeed, the National Literacy Strategy points out that successful teaching is characterized by high-quality, interactive talk.

So, encourage children to *think* as they read or listen, and draw on their prior knowledge of life and books in order to:

▲ predict outcomes: *What do you think will happen next? Why do you think that? What gave you a clue?*

▲ read 'between the lines' and discuss how the characters might be feeling and why; make comparisons with similar situations in their lives (For example, *Dogger* by Shirley Hughes (Red Fox) provokes responses about memories of real-life incidents and personal fears.)

▲ articulate their own feelings and put themselves in a character's shoes: *What would you have said or done in the same situation? Why?*

▲ read 'beyond the lines' and discuss the author's message (What is Jill Murphy telling us about female stereotypes or healthy eating in *A Piece of Cake* (Walker)?)

▲ explain what makes the book special and what they particularly like about it – authentic dialogue, expectations fulfilled, surprise twists in the plot (was anyone prepared for the ending of books such as *Princess Smartypants* by Babette Cole (Puffin)?)

▲ discuss the author's use of language – memorable phrases, rhythms, refrains, half-guessed meanings, figures of speech (Children love the rhymes and alliterations in Lynley Dodd's series of *Hairy Maclary* books, the rhythms and onomatopoeic words in the Caldecott Medal winner *A Story, A Story* by Gail Haley (Methuen).)

Resourcing the reading curriculum

There are plenty of books that foster children's development as thinking readers. Both cherished books from the past and significant contemporary books offer opportunities to debate important issues and develop literacy skills. If you look at the work of acclaimed authors, such as Rosemary Wells, Pat Hutchins, Anthony Browne, to name but a few, you find they have certain important characteristics in common, all of which help to motivate children to become engrossed with stories and get them 'hooked on books'. So, keep your eyes open for books that have:

▲ a strong narrative thrust (Children sit enthralled listening to *Dragon Slayer* by Rosemary Sutcliff (Red Fox) or *A Story, A Story*.)

▲ dilemmas that stimulate thought and raise vital questions. (What better than Anthony Browne's *Willy the Wimp* (Walker) to spark off concerns about gender stereotyping or bullying?)

▲ situations that stir the emotions and help us better understand ourselves and others (Sibling rivalry looms large in young children's minds – *Noisy Nora* by Rosemary Wells (Doubleday), *Peter's Chair* by Ezra Jack Keats (Red Fox) and *The Very Worst Monster* by Pat Hutchins (Red Fox) offer humorous ways to open up the debate.)

▲ stories that broaden experiences and present alternative points of view. (Jenny Wagner's *John Brown, Rose and the Midnight Cat* (Puffin) soon has the supporters of the old woman, the dog or the cat vying with each other to put their case.)

▲ fantasies that awaken the imagination. (*Come Away from the Water, Shirley* by John Burningham (Red Fox), and *Where the Wild Things Are* by Maurice Sendak (Picture Lions) lead to a multiplicity of interpretations from children as young as nursery age.)

▲ language used with flair (You need look no further than Ted Hughes' *The Iron Man* (Faber) for poetic language used at its best.)

The best resources in the world, however, cannot in themselves guarantee success. It is the impact of an enthusiastic teacher that is still the most persuasive force in any classroom.

SIMILARITIES AND DIFFERENCES

For the children to: describe story settings and incidents and relate them to their own experiences; identify and discuss characters' appearances, personalities, behaviour.

†† *Reading session: whole class. Children working in pairs. Final session: whole class.*

⏲ *Reading session: 20–25 minutes. Pair work session: 15–20 minutes. Feedback session: 15–20 minutes.*

Previous skills/knowledge needed

It would be helpful if children had some previous experience of listening and responding to stories read aloud to them in a large group, and experience of working co-operatively in pairs.

Key background information

This session is the first of three based on the book *Elmer: the Story of a Patchwork Elephant* by David McKee (Red Fox). It provides an opportunity for children to get to know and become involved with a lovable character. As he grows into a friend, children can begin to anticipate his actions and predict likely events in the story. They will begin to respond enthusiastically to the author's humour.

This first session is structured so as to comply with the requirements of the National Literacy Hour for work at text level.

Young children need the security of being accepted and valued by their peers, and often depend a great deal on being able to identify with their group. Children who do not conform to the features of the majority whether via race, culture, size, shape, ability, dress, accent, family pattern and so on, may find themselves isolated. This book provides an ideal opportunity for young children to explore and articulate their feelings about difference in an unthreatening way. Through discussion of a humorous story about an unusual young elephant coming to terms with looking different from the rest of the herd, children are encouraged to compare similar situations, actual or anticipated, in their own lives. This book should help all children to understand the concept of 'different but equal' that will enable them to celebrate difference as well as similarity. It is important to know your class well before attempting to discuss a sensitive issue such as this.

Preparation

Set up a display of as many of the Elmer books as you can find. Posters about the author would help to awaken children's interest. Tapes and video versions of the stories should be made available in the listening corner for children to enjoy at their leisure, on their own, with a friend or with a supportive adult. Prepare a list of 'prompt' questions about the setting of the story, what happens and the characters in the story.

Resources needed

Prompt questions, a flip chart or board, paper and writing materials, the *Elmer* books (including *Elmer: the Story of a Patchwork Elephant*), posters about the author (optional).

What to do

Read *Elmer: the Story of a Patchwork Elephant* to the class, pausing as appropriate to savour the humour and allow the children to predict what might happen next. At the end, encourage the children to comment freely and

spontaneously on the setting and events and the illustrations. Use your prompt questions here: these will help less experienced listeners to make a contribution, and may stimulate further questions and comments from others.

Guide the children to relate the characters and events to their own experience by asking questions like: *Why was Elmer feeling miserable? How was he different from the other elephants? What did he decide to do about it? Did that help? How did Elmer feel at the end of the story? What did the other elephants think of Elmer?* Finally, ask the children if they thought the story had a good ending, what Elmer had learned by the end of the story, what they liked best about the story and why.

Move from the situation in the book to real life – do we have patchwork people? No! But, do all people look alike? With the children's help, make a list on the flip chart of all the possible differences between people, such as height, weight, hair colour and style, shape of face, eye colour and shape, gender, race, religion, family pattern, lifestyle, clothes, food, interests, favourite subjects at school, voice, accent, dialect. Remind the children to think about friends, family members, teachers, neighbours, famous people.

Discuss with the class any incidents when they, like Elmer, have felt uncomfortable or left out, when they have been called names, bullied or laughed at, for instance for wearing glasses or being overweight. Talk with the children about how they felt on such occasions then discuss positive ways of helping people to feel valued, ways of welcoming people into a group. It is only fair to acknowledge that we all have days when we fall out with our friends and say things that we do not really mean.

Divide the class into pairs to list helpful ways of overcoming feelings of anger or disappointment, and ways of sorting out any disagreements between friends.

Gather the class together after about 15 minutes and write all the children's ideas on the flip chart.

Finally, you could talk about the *similarities* between people, such as the need for friends and family; attention and success; enjoyment and fun; shelter, food and warmth. Highlight the fact that the most important aspect about people is not what they look like, but how they behave towards each other.

Suggestion(s) for extension
Confident writers could make a poster listing all the things they can do to promote a harmonious classroom atmosphere.

Suggestion(s) for support
All children should be able to join in this reading activity as the prompt questions will allow everyone to contribute.

Assessment opportunities
Note the children's level of response to the story, their involvement in the discussion about the issues involved and their articulacy in putting across their viewpoints.

Opportunities for IT
Posters illustrating events or characters in the story could be designed with a DTP package. 'Developing Tray' activities could be devised based on the text of the story.

Display ideas
Scenes from the story could be painted and mounted as a frieze for the classroom.

Other aspects of the English PoS covered
Speaking and listening – 1a, c; 2b.
Writing – 1b, c; 2a, c, d, e.

WHO'S TALKING?

For the children to: identify speech marks in reading, understand their purposes and use terms correctly; investigate and recognize ways of presenting text (speech bubbles and so on).

†† *Introductory session: whole class. Children working in groups. Final session: whole class.*

⊕ *Introductory session: 20–25 minutes. Group work session: 20 minutes. Feedback session: 15 minutes.*

Previous skills/knowledge needed

Children should already have done the previous activity, 'Similarities and differences', and thereby be acquainted with *Elmer: the Story of a Patchwork Elephant*. It would be helpful if children had already been introduced to speech bubbles.

Key background information

Children need to know that there are certain marked differences between speech and writing. For instance when we read, we cannot hear voices as we can when we listen to someone talking. So, writers have to let us know when someone is talking. Close observation of comics and texts, drawing children's attention to speech bubbles and speech marks will help children to understand the conventions for punctuating direct speech.

This activity focuses on work at sentence level.

Preparation

Collect a number of suitable comics and books that use speech bubbles and speech marks. On a large sheet of paper, draw a picture of Elmer with a speech bubble issuing from his trunk.

Resources needed

A copy of *Elmer: the Story of a Patchwork Elephant*, a flip chart or board, a large sheet of paper (see 'Preparation'), writing materials, a copy of photocopiable sheet 100 for each child, a copy of sheet 101 for more confident readers and writers.

What to do

Introduce or remind the children of the term **speech bubbles** and show some examples from the collection of comics you have gathered together. Write 'Good Morning' in the speech bubble on the prepared drawing of Elmer. The story of Elmer should already be familiar to the children from a previous session, when the meanings of the text were explored and a full discussion of the issues undertaken.

Point out to the children that there are no speech bubbles in the text of the story and yet we can tell who is talking. *How does the author manage that?* Explain to the children that you will read the story again and that this time you want them to concentrate on what Elmer *says*. Support your listeners by exaggerating the intonation of the spoken words and perhaps varying the voices for the

different speakers, if possible.

After the reading, scribe on the flip chart or board a few examples of direct speech from the book, such as 'Hello, day'; 'Good morning Elmer'. Highlight the **speech marks** that signal to the reader, in the middle of the **continuous text**, the words actually spoken. Compare the convention with that of speech bubbles in comics where, instead of continuous text, there are **illustrations**. Draw children's attention to the clues in the book that accompany the spoken words to tell us who is speaking, for example 'said', 'asked', 'called'.

The children now work in groups. Hand out photocopiable sheet 100 and explain to the children that they have to supply the words the elephants might be saying to each other in the speech bubbles provided.

When the groups have finished, briefly share some of the work and write it on the flip chart or board, before recapping on the use of speech bubbles and speech marks. Remind the children to stress the intonation of spoken words when they read stories aloud to each other.

Suggestion(s) for extension

As well as having to supply the words for the speech bubbles, some children could also be expected to write out on photocopiable sheet 101 the alternative version using speech marks.

Encourage confident readers and writers to continue a list of all the ways you can greet people and to use as many languages and dialects as possible.

Suggestion(s) for support

Mixed ability groups would support those children whose handwriting skills are not yet well developed. Never equate poor small motor control with a dearth of ideas!

Assessment opportunities

Note children's understanding of the difference in usage between speech bubbles and speech marks and their ability to explain it clearly.

Opportunities for IT

Rules for punctuating direct speech could be drawn up on the computer. Software packages to practise the correct use of punctuation abound, and those children who are keen on linguistic exercises might benefit. Bear in mind, however, that many children find such decontextualized practice very tedious and fail to transfer the learning to active use in their daily writing.

Display ideas

You could mount a display of a parade of large, painted elephants with speech bubbles attached, perhaps with a border of the same utterances written as sentences with speech marks.

Other aspects of the English PoS covered

Speaking and listening – 1a, c.
Writing – 2c.

Reference to photocopiable sheets

Photocopiable sheet 100 provides children with the opportunity to generate speech for speech bubbles.

Sheet 101 is intended for more experienced children to incorporate a translation of these utterances into direct speech sentences using the correct punctuation, that is, speech marks.

ALLITERATION

For the children to: consolidate the discrimination of initial phonemes; identify alliteration in known words.

†† *Introductory session: whole class. Children working in groups. Final session: whole class.*

⏲ *Introductory session: 20 minutes. Group work session: 20 minutes. Feedback session: 10–15 minutes.*

Previous skills/knowledge needed

Children should already be acquainted with the book, *Elmer: the Story of a Patchwork Elephant* and have worked through the previous two activities. It would be helpful if children had encountered all the letters of the alphabet and their associated sounds.

Key background information

Young children have a natural ear for language and can recognize rhyme and alliteration from an early age. This activity provides an opportunity to develop children's phonological awareness, which research has shown to be a contributing factor to children's success as readers. It involves work at word level.

Preparation

Write out on a large sheet of paper, board or OHT, several examples of alliterative sentences that you have come across in the recent books you have read to the class, or in rhymes they know well.

Resources needed

Examples of alliterative sentences, OHP (optional), a copy of *Elmer: the Story of a Patchwork Elephant*, a flip chart or board, paper, writing and drawing materials.

What to do

Read aloud to the class the first page of the story, then say aloud with emphasis, 'a herd of happy elephants'. Ask the children what strikes them about that phrase. If necessary, point out the repetition of the **h** sounds at the beginning of the words. Explain to the children that writers sometimes repeat sounds in this way to create a pleasing effect, and that it is called **alliteration**.

Show the children the sheet of examples you prepared earlier, and read them aloud together so as to hear the repetition of the sounds. Then, focusing on the example in *Elmer*, brainstorm other alliterative phrases using the same words as a starting point, for example 'a herd of happy heiffers', 'a herd of happy hedgehogs', 'a herd of happy hamsters', 'a herd of happy hippopotami', 'a herd of happy hogs', 'a herd of happy horses', and so on. List them all on the flip chart.

Divide the class where possible into groups of similar competency to work on these differentiated tasks.

To consolidate learning, those groups needing support could copy out in neat the phrases on the flip chart the class has produced ready for display, and perhaps draw pictures to go with them. Encourage attention to detail in the illustrations, such as texture of fur or feathers, as well as in handwriting formation.

Other groups could extend the phrases generated by the class by adding verbs to describe the action the animals took, for example 'a herd of happy hamsters hurried to the house'.

Once the work has been completed, gather the class together again and encourage the children to show and/or read out their suggestions.

Suggestion(s) for extension and support

The differentiated tasks in this activity will ensure that all children can complete the activity at an appropriate level.

Assessment opportunities

Note children's ability to recognize initial letter sounds and to recognize and use the term 'alliteration'.

Opportunities for IT

Collections of alliterative sentences could be word-processed in the form of a collective poem.

Display ideas

A 'Let's celebrate sounds' display could be produced, with illustrations in vivid pastels of all the animals in herds and the alliterative phrases used as headings.

Other aspects of the English PoS covered

Speaking and listening – 1a; 2b; 3b.
Writing – 2d, e.

TEXT COMPLETION

For the children to: predict story endings, such as unfinished extracts; read aloud their finished stories to the class.

†† *Introductory session: whole class. Group writing session. Reading aloud session: whole class.*

🕐 *Introductory session: 15–20 minutes. Group writing session: 20–25 minutes. Reading aloud session: 15–20 minutes.*

Previous skills/knowledge needed

It would be helpful if children already had some experience of talking about what might happen next in a story, as it is being read to them, as well as discussing alternative endings for stories.

Key background information

John Burningham is an author and illustrator of renown, whose work is an embodiment of all the criteria we mentioned in the introduction to this section to ensure a rattling good read. His books are particularly useful for reinforcing the importance of the illustrations in a text, not only to complement the text, but also to carry the narrative and extend the text. They are ideal for encouraging children to savour illustrations and to learn to 'read' pictures by picking up the clues offered to the reader by the illustrator.

This activity is centred on the book *Borka: the Adventures of a Goose With No Feathers* (Red Fox), which deals with rejection, making new friends, and the acceptance of an alternative lifestyle. We follow the trials

and tribulations of a young goose, born with no feathers, who cannot fly and so cannot migrate south in winter with the rest of her family. Eventually, she finds a new family and friends… and lives happily ever after.

The activity involves work at text level.

Preparation

Mount a display of John Burningham books, together with any biographical material about the author, posters from publishers, dust jackets of books, and so on. Make it look as appealing as possible to whet children's appetites.

Resources needed

Books by John Burningham (including a copy of *Borka: the Adventures of a Goose With No Feathers*), a flip chart or board, paper and writing materials.

What to do

Tell the children that they are going to meet a new author and illustrator today called John Burningham. Show them the front cover of the book. Get the children thinking about possible scenarios by asking them what the title and cover suggest to them. What do they think might happen in this story? Have they ever come across a goose with no feathers before?

Read the story to the class up to the point where Borka's family fly off for the winter, leaving her behind.

Firstly, encourage the children to make their own personal responses to what they have heard so far. Then, explain that the class is now going to take over the role of author to complete the story, based on what has gone before. Ask the children to share a few initial ideas with

the friend next to them for a few minutes. Take suggestions from them in turn and scribe them on the flip chart, praising appropriate, thoughtful, creative ideas.

Divide the class into appropriate groups for the differentiated writing task of completing the story.

Competent writers can work individually on their story within their group and be asked to proof-read their work before the plenary session. Children with less experience in writing should work in small groups to complete a shared piece of writing, with an adult helper as scribe if necessary.

Remind children before they begin of the features that make a good story, such as logical sequence of ideas, lively style, interesting vocabulary, variety of sentence length and construction, perhaps humour or pathos.

When the stories are completed, gather as a class so that the children can read their versions to each other. Remind them about audibility, clarity, expression and emphasis, pauses and changes in speed, tone and volume when reading aloud.

Suggestion(s) for extension and support
All children should be able to complete this activity at an appropriate level through the differentiated writing task.

Assessment opportunities
Note children's ability to handle narrative structure and to complete a story in a coherent way. You can monitor their writing skills while they are composing, and their confidence and reading aloud skills in the final session.

Opportunities for IT
The children's writing could be produced for display using DTP.

Display ideas
The story starter, either surrounded by the different children's endings or used at the beginning of a frieze, would make an interesting display for other classes to read.

Other aspects of the Pos covered
Speaking and listening – 1a; 2b.
Writing – 1b; 2a, b, c, d, e.

COMPLEX SENTENCES

For the children to: be more aware of grammatical structures, namely relative clauses; generate complex sentences using relative clauses, modelled on the text.

†† *Introductory session: whole class. Children working in groups. Feedback session: whole class.*

⏱ *Introductory session: 15 minutes. Group work session: 20 minutes. Feedback session: 15 minutes.*

Previous skills/knowledge needed
It would be helpful if children were already used to discussions focusing on language use, and if they had completed the previous activity, 'Text completion'.

Key background information
Syntactical cues provide one of the three main strategies to readers in their progress towards fluency. This session provides an opportunity for children to focus on aspects of syntax to expand their knowledge and develop their understanding in this area. It involves work at sentence level and moves children on from simple sentences, or sentences linked by 'and' or 'then', to complex sentences, including a relative clause.

Resources needed
A copy of *Borka: the Adventures of a Goose With No Feathers*, a flip chart or board, writing paper and writing materials.

What to do

Gather the whole class together and tell them that you are going to focus on one specific element of the Borka story. Ask the children if they can remember how Mr Plumster kept the eggs safe in the nest. Read from the part that tells how he guarded the nest to keep it safe from predators: 'He hissed at anything that came near the nest.' Together make a collection of alternative actions that Mr Plumster could have taken, using the same sentence construction and changing only the last part of the sentence. For example: 'He hissed at anything that flew over the nest', 'He hissed at anything that passed by the nest', 'He hissed at anything that floated up to the nest', 'He hissed at anything that swam close to the nest'. List them on the flip chart or board for the children to refer to later.

Now divide the class into appropriate groups to carry out the following writing tasks.

Ask the most able language users to generate similar sentences with a humorous touch, perhaps about their own dad instead of about Borka's dad. For instance: 'My dad shouts at anyone that comes near our house', 'My dad bellows at anyone that walks past our house', 'My dad throws tomatoes at anyone that opens our front gate', 'My dad makes the dog growl at anyone that knocks on our front door'.

Children who are less secure in their syntactical understanding could be asked to write out the sentences generated in the class session, but replacing the main verb with an alternative. For example: 'He squawked at anything

that flew over the nest', 'He snapped at anything that passed by the nest', 'He flew at anything that floated up to the nest', 'He flapped his wings at anything that swam close to the nest'.

After about 20 minutes, regroup as a class so that the children can read out to each other what they have done. To round off the session, you could introduce alternative words for 'that' at the start of the relative clause, that is, 'which' and 'who'.

Suggestion(s) for extension and support

Assigning children to an appropriate group for the syntax exercise means that all the children will be able to complete this activity.

Assessment opportunities

Note children's ability to handle the sentence construction and generate further examples of their own, as well as their fluency when reading their work aloud to their peers.

Opportunities for IT

Children could use a computer instead of hand-writing their sentences for display.

Display ideas

During the week the children could prepare their sentences for display with decorative borders and appropriate illustrations. They could incorporate speech bubbles supplying Dad's actual words or Mr Plumster's 'squawk', 'hiss' and so on.

Other aspects of the English PoS covered

Speaking and listening – 1a; 2a.
Writing – 2b; 3a.

OPPOSITES

For the children to: explore antonyms; collect and discuss differences in meaning.

†† *Introductory session: whole class. Children working individually, in pairs or groups. Feedback session: whole class.*

🕐 *Introductory session: 20 minutes. Individual/pair/group work session: 15–20 minutes. Feedback session: 15 minutes.*

Previous skills/knowledge needed

It would be helpful if the children had some previous experience of looking closely at words and meanings, and are familiar with the book *Borka: the Adventures of a Goose With No Feathers*.

Key background information

This session provides an opportunity to develop children's interest in words and their meanings. Raising children's awareness of language and encouraging them to look closely at words increases their phonological awareness and improves their grapho-phonic skills, as well as fostering discussion about precise meanings.

This activity involves work at text and word level.

Preparation

Photocopy the requisite number of copies of sheets 102 and 103 to suit your class's needs.

Resources needed

A flip chart or board, writing materials, copies of photocopiable sheets 102 and 103, a copy of *Borka: the Adventures of a Goose With No Feathers*.

What to do

Explain to the class that today you will be investigating vocabulary connected with the weather. Ask the children if they remember any weather words from the book about Borka. Prompt with clues, such as: *How did Borka feel at night with no feathers to protect her? How did the geese know that it was time to migrate south?*

As well as noting all the relevant words in the text, talk with the children about weather forecasts they might have seen on television. Write the collection of weather words the class offer on the flip chart or board, remembering to include words for all seasons – rain, snow, drizzle, hail, sleet, frost, cold, freezing, wet, foggy, misty, cloudy, dull, overcast, showery, mild, dry, clear, bright, sunny, hot, sweltering, scorching, muggy, steamy.

Hand out copies of photocopiable sheets 102 and 103 to appropriate children.

Children with a well-established repertoire of weather vocabulary will be able to progress immediately to using photocopiable sheet 103 to generate similes, such as 'It was as hot as the Iron Man's anvil', 'It was as dark as a bottomless pit', 'It was as muddy as a Louisiana swamp'. These children can work individually or in pairs.

Where help with developing vocabulary is needed, children should work with the support of a friend or in a small group on photocopiable sheet 102. The children decide which word is opposite in meaning to the one given in the left-hand column.

Explain what they have to do in each case and do an example or two from each sheet to get the children going.

When the work has been completed, gather the class together and ask children to read out their contributions to their peers. Write a selection on the flip chart. Discuss any difficulties encountered by the children working on opposites: for instance: *Were some words difficult to find exact opposites for? Could some words have been used twice?* Praise the efforts of children who have been able to avoid clichés and generate innovative similes.

Suggestion(s) for extension and support

The differentiated task on antonyms/similes and differences in meaning allows each child to accomplish the activity at an appropriate level.

Assessment opportunities

Note children's ability to find opposites and their understanding that there is not always only one clear answer, and sometimes there may not be one at all. Monitor the facility of the more competent group of language users in their search for creative similes that avoid the obvious clichés.

Opportunities for IT

Follow-up work on weather reports could be produced using IT, as could a presentation of the children's collections of opposites and similes.

Display ideas

The collections mentioned above would make a suitable focus for a small 'Looking at language' display.

Other aspects of the English PoS covered

Speaking and listening – 1a; 3b.
Writing – 2d, e; 3b

What's the weather like?

Name _____ Date _____

▲ Read carefully, then finish the sentences below in as interesting a way as you can.

The weather was as wet as _____

It was as calm as _____

It is as clear as _____

The sun was as bright as _____

The day was as dull as _____

It felt as cold as _____

The air is as hot as _____

The sky was as dark as _____

bright	
sunny	
wet	
mild	
calm	
clear	
freezing	
fine	

Reference to photocopiable sheets

Drawing on the vocabulary generated in the whole class session, sheet 102 asks children to select words that mean the opposite of the ones given.

Sheet 103 requires children to create similes using the weather words from the initial session.

REAL AND IMAGINED LIVES

For the children to: discuss familiar story themes, linked to their own experiences.

†† *Introductory session: whole class. Children working in groups. Presentation sessions: small groups.*

⏱ *Introductory session: 20 minutes. Group work session: 15–20 minutes. Presentation sessions: 15 minutes each.*

Previous skills/knowledge needed

It would be helpful if children had considerable previous experience in hearing stories read aloud and talking about them with each other. It would be interesting for comparison if the children had already come across other books with a pig as the central character, such as *Charlotte's Web* by EB White (Puffin) and/or the Mary Rayner books, such as *Garth Pig and the Ice Cream Lady* (Macmillan).

Key background information

This session provides an opportunity for children to respond emotionally to the content of a story, and to make comparisons between the events in the book and ones that have happened to them or their friends or family in real life. All the animals in *A Medal for Poppy* (Rose Impey, Orchard) are afraid of something or other, but they wrongly believe that Poppy pig is an exception. This book allows you to revisit the issue of fears in a rather humorous way. Here, irrational fears are accepted as inevitable, and the trick is to learn how to live with them. It involves children in work at text level.

Work at sentence level could also spring from using the book, by focusing on different grammatical constructions, such as:

Fancy being afraid of...,

No one seemed to notice...,

Poppy wasn't afraid of bright lights or loud noises or being alone in the dark.

Work at word level is equally possible. For instance words for animal young ('duckling', 'chick', and so on); phonological awareness (*oo/sh/ck*).

Preparation

Display a collection of the *Animal Crackers* series of books by Rose Impey and Shoo Raynor (Orchard) and encourage children to browse through them at their leisure or read them with friends.

Resources needed

A copy of *A Medal for Poppy*, writing materials.

What to do

Introduce *A Medal for Poppy* to the class and ask for suggestions as to why the children think that Poppy might win a medal. Draw on children's experiences with other stories about pigs that you have shared together: *Why did Wilbur win a medal at the show? Might Poppy be eligible for the same sort of prize?*

Then, read the story to the class, savouring the humorous comments in speech bubbles, and stressing the words, 'That's what I call brave: knowing what you're afraid of, but not letting it get the better of you.' When the children have responded spontaneously to the story, discuss this view with them. Ask them about their own fears and, together, consider ways of coping.

Divide the class into appropriate groups to prepare a presentation of the story. Confident children could prepare a dramatic presentation of the story, while confident readers could prepare for a shared/choral reading of other stories in the *Animal Crackers* series to present to the class later in the week. Less confident readers could prepare a shared retelling of the Poppy story to present to the class. Then, during the week call on the groups in turn to perform for the rest of the class.

Suggestion(s) for extension and support

The story presentation task is differentiated to allow all children to participate at an appropriate level.

Assessment opportunities

Note children's readiness to discuss their feelings in the initial whole-group situation, and their reading aloud and/or story retelling or drama skills in the presentation sessions.

Opportunities for IT

A DTP package could be used to transform the suggestions generated in the whole-class session for coping with fears into a large-scale poster.

Display ideas

The collection of *Animal Crackers* books should be on display during the activity and while the presentations are being made in sessions during the week.

Other aspects of the English PoS covered

Speaking and listening – 1a, c, d; 2b.

NARRATIVE STRUCTURE

For the children to: develop knowledge of narrative structure; learn terms such as 'narrative', 'character', 'setting', 'plot'.

†† *Introductory oral session: whole class. Children working in pairs. Feedback session: whole class.*

🕐 *Introductory session: 20 minutes. Pair work session: 20 minutes. Feedback session: 15–20 minutes.*

Previous skills/knowledge needed

Children need to have a solid background in listening to and talking about a range of different stories.

Key background information

As children become more familiar with a range of stories, it is important to draw their attention to the common features that recur in this particular genre. You need to point out the main stages in a narrative structure that unfold in a chronological pattern:

▲ The beginning

This sets the scene for the reader by establishing the time and the place, and introduces the characters: 'Once upon a time, long, long ago, in a faraway land, there lived …'

▲ The middle

This is the main body of the story, with a series of events that often pose problems for the main characters to resolve: 'One day, on her way to market, the peasant's daughter came upon a…' There is often a final resolution when the hero or heroine faces the ultimate challenge

and overcomes the last hurdle: 'With one mighty thrust, he plunged his sword into the dragon's heart and it fell dead at his feet.'

▲ The end

This is when the reader finds out how the story finishes and what the future has in store for the main characters: 'And together they rode back to the prince's palace, where they lived happily ever after.'

This activity is centred on the book *Anancy and Mr Drybone* by Fiona French (Francis Lincoln), which is a retelling of a traditional tale based on characters from Caribbean and West African folk-tales. It is an exemplar of one successful approach, but any story that you enjoy and that the children are familiar with can lend itself to this sort of exploration. It would be preferable if the children were already familiar with the book before this session.

The activity involves work at text level, although the book also provides possibilities for work at sentence level (looking at 'but' clauses, for instance, modelled on usage in the text: 'My evening suit is at the cleaners right now, *but* you can borrow my jogging suit.'), and at word level (exploring superlatives, for instance, modelled on the usage in the text: '"Anancy," she choked, "that is the weird*est* get-up I ever did see."').

Preparation

Collect and display a range of books by the same author, Fiona French, a range of traditional tales from around the world, together with your class's favourite stories, and perhaps the latest narrative acquisitions to your bookshelf – any rattling good stories that the children will enjoy.

Ensure that you have read this story to the children at least once before this focused session.

You will need sufficient copies of photocopiable sheets 104 and 105 to suit the needs of each child in your class.

Resources needed
A copy of *Anancy and Mr Dry-bone*, a range of books as described above, copies of photocopiable sheets 104 and 105 for each child as appropriate, a flip chart or board, writing and drawing materials.

What to do
Look through the book with the class, allowing the children plenty of time to savour the illustrations. (As an accomplished artist first and foremost, Fiona French's illustrations are every bit as important as the text.) Encourage the children to recap their favourite moments from the story.

Now, ask the children to listen carefully as you read the story to them to distinguish where the story starts and ends, and the sequence of the main events that make up the plot. Then discuss with the children the key factors in this narrative structure:

▲ **The beginning** of the story – when the main characters, Mr Dry-bone, Anancy and Miss Louise are introduced, and the setting where the illustrations of the animals, house, flowers, trees enhance the text to evoke the atmosphere of the Caribbean.

▲ **The middle** – enumerate in order the various attempts by Mr Dry-bone and Anancy to make Miss Louise laugh, then the final resolution when Anancy wins the contest.

▲ **The end** – 'So Anancy married Miss Louise, and they all lived happily ever after.'

Explain to the class that they are going to work in pairs and look at the structure of a story. Each pair will choose a story from the selection of books you have provided, and their task is to locate the beginning, middle and end of their chosen story, and record that on their sheet.

Competent readers and writers can use the framework on photocopiable sheet 105 to record in their own words how their story begins, develops and ends. Children requiring more help can use the storyboard framework on photocopiable sheet 104 to write what they can and draw appropriate illustrations to indicate the beginning, middle and end of their stories.

Gather the class together when the work has been completed to share some of the children's findings. Highlight the key teaching points about narrative structure, and consolidate the new terminology introduced. As a closing activity, you could ask children to talk about narrative structure in different media, such as in a favourite film or television programme.

Suggestion(s) for extension and support
The task of exploring a basic narrative structure can be undertaken at the correct level of competence by all the children; by writing alone, by drawing or a combination of the two.

Assessment opportunities
Note children's understanding of the terms introduced and their developing knowledge of narrative structure.

Opportunities for IT

A storyboard format could be used for children to map out the structure of their favourite stories.

Display ideas

A collection of story books, as described earlier, should be available for browsing as well as for specific use during the session. The completed storyboards should also be displayed, perhaps enlarged and divided into beginnings, middles and endings.

Other aspects of the English PoS covered

Speaking and listening – 1a, c; 2b; 3b.
Writing – 1c; 2a, b, c, d, e.

Reference to photocopiable sheets

Photocopiable sheets 104 and 105 provide differentiated ways of representing the basic stages of narrative structure, either through words or drawings.

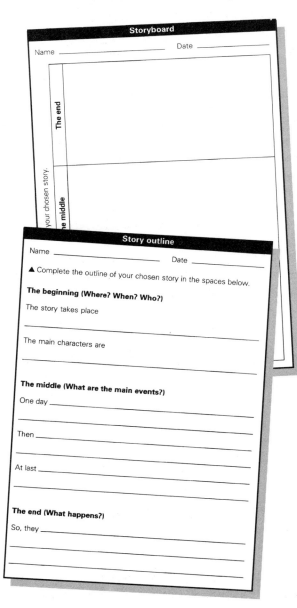

SHORT STORY GENRE

For the children to: explore the similarities and differences between two literary genres, novels and short stories.

†† *Reading sessions: whole class. Introductory oral session: whole class. Children working in groups. Feedback session: whole class.*

🕐 *Reading sessions: 15 minutes each. Introductory session: 5 minutes. Group work session: 20 minutes. Feedback session: 15 minutes.*

Previous skills/knowledge needed

It is expected that children will have had experience of listening to and/or reading novels.

Key background information

This activity provides an opportunity for work at text level. It introduces children to a new literary genre, the short story, to highlight its characteristic features and make comparisons with novels. Salient factors the children might comment on in the session could include:

▲ both follow a narrative structure with a beginning, middle and end

▲ there is a list of contents in a book of short stories; a list of chapters in a novel

▲ short stories can be read in any order

▲ you don't have to read all the stories in a collection – you can pick and choose

▲ you find out what happens in the end more quickly in a short story

▲ you don't need so much reading stamina for short stories

▲ you can read a short story more easily on your own

▲ you can have a range of different types of stories in one book

▲ you can have a range of different writers in a book of short stories

▲ short stories offer a good model for children's own writing

▲ in novels you enjoy the suspense at the end of a chapter

▲ in a novel there's more space to set the scene in detail at the beginning

▲ you have time to get to know the characters really well in a novel

▲ sometimes you want a story to build up slowly and go on for a long time.

Rose Impey's collection, *First Class* (Orchard) makes a good starting point. A softback book with familiar picture book elements, it introduces children to short stories in a non-threatening way. The subject matter stems directly from children's everyday experiences, yet Rose Impey does not offer the conventional cosy images you might expect. Instead, she challenges the *status quo* and received opinions; she asks important questions, especially about sexist stereotypes and the role of girls. Under a humorous guise, her books always start children thinking and debating really valid issues of contemporary life.

Preparation
You will need to read the six stories one at a time to the class over a week or so, encouraging the class to respond fully to each one. Ask them to make comparisons with what is on offer in the school in the book and in their own school.

Arrange a display of a variety of novels and short-story collections. Select one or two of each genre to show in the introductory session.

Resources needed
Previously selected books a, a copy of *First Class* by Rose Impey, large sheets of paper, writing materials, copies of photocopiable sheet 106 for children needing support.

What to do
When all the stories have been read and discussed with the class, tell the children that you want them to work in groups to list all the similarities and all the differences between a book of short stories like this one and the novels you have read to them recently. Show one or two of each genre from the collection you have gathered for display to start the ball rolling. Ask questions like: *Do they have a similar narrative structure, with a beginning, middle and end? How much importance is attached to setting the scene? How well do we get to know the main characters?*

Divide the class into groups to draw up independent lists of the features of the two literary genres. Depending on the level of experience of your class, you may want to organize mixed ability groups to create posters on large sheets of paper. Alternatively, you may prefer to arrange differentiated groups and offer photocopiable sheet 106 to those children who need more support, either with the ideas or with writing them down.

When the work is completed, ask the groups to show and read their posters or their tick-lists to the rest of the class. Comment constructively on the children's findings and discuss any discrepancies. You could take a vote as to who prefers novels and who short stories.

You could round off the session by saying that most of us like reading *both*, and that our choice at any given time might depend on how we are feeling, how much time we have, where we are, who the author is, who recommended the book to us, how interesting the front cover and the blurb are, and so on.

Suggestion(s) for extension and support
The differentiated task of exploring the similarities and differences between novels and short stories allows all children to complete the activity according to their own level of competence.

Assessment opportunities
Note children's understanding of the similarities and differences between the two genres and their ability to recall such features.

Opportunities for IT
Children could follow up the activity by 'publishing' a class collection of short stories about their own school, modelled on *First Class*. Alternatively, some children may like to publish a short story collection centred on a common theme, such as family, friends, pets, holidays.

Display ideas
An initial display of novels and short stories should be prepared, as suggested earlier. Children's finished posters detailing the features of novels and short stories, could also be displayed.

Other aspects of the English PoS covered
Speaking and listening – 1a, c; 2b; 3b.
Writing – 1b, c; 2a.

Reference to photocopiable sheet
Photocopiable sheet 106 offers a framework for children who need some support to explore the different features of short stories and novels. Ideas are supplied in a tick-list format, which requires less writing stamina and handwriting skill.

Novels v short stories

Name _____ Date _____

▲ Read the statements carefully, then put a tick in the column you think each one applies to.

Comments	Novels	Short stories
The story has a beginning, middle and end.		
There is a list of contents.		
There is a list of chapters.		
You can read it in any order.		
You don't have to read the whole book.		
It is easy to read on your own.		
You get a variety of stories in one book.		
I can write stories like this.		
You can get a variety of authors in one book.		
It is exciting to look forward to the next chapter.		
The writer can take more time to set the scene.		
There's more space for details.		
You have time to get to know the characters well.		
The tension builds up as the story develops.		

I like to read _____

because _____

Poetry

It all starts with listening. Children need to hear poetry read to them from an early age, progressing from the action songs and finger plays of babyhood to nursery rhymes and short rhyming stories that are quickly learned by heart without any effort. Children delight in the familiar and need to hear a wide range of vernacular poetry, but that repertoire of the familiar needs to keep expanding, so new poems should be introduced regularly. Class reading, reciting, choral chanting and setting poems to music should be ongoing experiences in every classroom. Listening to tapes and making some with one's own favourite poems should play a big part too; likewise, creating class anthologies, justifying choices and writing reviews. Taking poetry into drama, at times with puppets, masks, costumes and percussion, adds an extra dimension.

Poetry goes hand in hand with an appreciation of language and a growing awareness of its potential, with a love of playing with words in word-games, puns, jokes, sayings, figurative expressions, similes and metaphors. All these experiences will help to ensure that the next generation of children is spared the millstone belief that poetry is alien, difficult and for only the rare few.

Writing poems has an important role to play too, especially if this is followed up by preparing and presenting them to an audience and making a class publication. The intimate experiences of family life and close personal relationships are as good a starting point as any. Children need to be familiar with the full range of poetic styles and forms before they can be expected to feel comfortable writing in a particular genre. Modelling on known structures provides a highly successful way into writing poetry.

LISTEN AND LEARN

For the children to: listen carefully to a poem being read aloud; learn by heart and recite a poem with predictable and repeated sound patterns; recognize and experiment with a repetitive rhythmical pattern.

†† *Oral session: whole class. Children working in groups.*

🕐 *Oral session: 45–60 minutes, two sessions of 25–30 minutes, or three sessions of 15–20 minutes. Group work session: 15 minutes.*

Previous skills/knowledge needed

None is essential, but previous experiences will affect the organization of the session (see 'What to do'). Children with little or no previous experience in this area would benefit from a gradual build-up over several sessions – talking and reading; reading and reciting; reciting and adding rhythmical accompaniment – before taping the choral reading of the poem.

Key background information

The importance of developing an ear for language and for building up a repertoire of poems known off by heart is well documented: enjoyment in wordplay helps to develop children's interest in and knowledge of rhyme, rhythm, alliteration, assonance and meanings. Confidence is enhanced by reading aloud together and by reciting chorally as a group.

Preparation

Copy onto a large sheet of paper or OHT for display on a flip chart or OHP the traditional poem 'A parade! A parade!' on photocopiable sheet 107. It has a strong rhythmical beat and a repeating refrain that will lend itself easily to learning off by heart.

Collect some books about carnivals and parades, such as *Nini at the carnival* by Eric Carle (Penguin).

Resources needed

A tape recorder and cassette, some percussion instruments, books about carnivals and parades, photocopiable page 107, a flip chart or OHP, art and writing materials, a copy of photocopiable sheet 108 for each child.

What to do

With the whole class gathered together on the mat, ask the children if any of them have watched a parade – perhaps in their local town or when on holiday here or abroad. Maybe a special carnival takes place locally to celebrate Mardi Gras or August Bank Holiday? Maybe they have been to London to see the Lord Mayor's procession? Maybe they have seen a circus parade on television or news items about carnivals in Rio de Janeiro or Notting Hill? Tell them that often parades have a religious significance, such as Oberammergau in Bavaria, kermis events in the Netherlands and France, saints' days in Spain,

the Inti Raymi festival in Peru that commemorates old Inca traditions from the past. Sometimes parades celebrate national events, such as Independence Day.

Discuss in more detail the children's memories of parades: Which animals were on view? Did they see any clowns? Acrobats? Were there any floats? What can they remember about the costumes people were wearing? Were there any musicians or dancers? You could read the book *Nini at the carnival* and discuss making costumes – the time it takes, the cost of materials, the skills, the planning.

Read out the poem 'A parade! A parade!', exaggerating the rhythms and keeping the beat with a handclap. Read it again, this time encouraging the children to join in with the handclapping. Then ask them to join you in reading from the enlarged version of the poem, while keeping the clapping accompaniment going. As the children gain confidence, you could add other rhythmical accompaniments, such as finger clicking, toe tapping, body sway and percussion. Round off the session by taping the class's choral reading of the poem, accompanied by the body percussion sounds.

To develop children's awareness of rhythmical patterns and rhyming words, children work in small groups and complete photocopiable sheet 108.

As follow-up activities, the children could write out the poem in their best handwriting, with appropriate border decorations. They could write about parades they have been to or seen on film or conduct a library hunt for poems and books on the same theme to share in class.

Suggestion(s) for extension

Ask the children to work in groups to choose a favourite poem and prepare to recite it to the class, with handclapping or body percussion sounds of their choice.

Suggestion(s) for support

In the whole class session, less experienced children could be asked either to join in with the reading or the clapping, or to join in only with the refrain.

When working with the photocopiable sheet 108, less confident children could read the sentences aloud with an adult, before supplying the missing words.

Opportunities for IT

Children could experiment with different fonts and text features on a computer, to produce the poem for display on the classroom wall.

Assessment opportunities

There are opportunities to note the children's ability to read from the enlarged text, the speed at which they learn the poem by heart, their awareness of the rhyming and rhythmical patterns in the poem, their facility at keeping the beat and reciting the poem with expression.

Display ideas

The class could make a frieze about parades or carnivals with songs, poems and personal accounts, as well as large-scale paintings and drawings.

Other aspects of the English PoS covered

Speaking and listening – 1a, c; 2a, b.
Writing – 2e.

Reference to photocopiable sheets

Photocopiable sheet 107 provides a copy of the poem 'A parade! A parade!' ready for enlargement to use in the whole-class session.

Photocopiable sheet 108 provides a cloze procedure activity for children to complete that requires them to keep to a set rhythmical pattern and to generate words that rhyme.

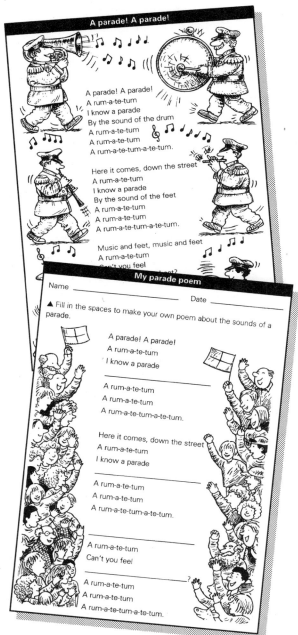

KEEP LISTENING AND LEARNING

For the children to: extend their knowledge of types of poetry; enjoy poetry containing patterned language; recognize and experiment with sound patterns and rhyme; read and learn a humorous animal poem.

†† *Whole class.*

⏱ *35–40 minutes.*

Previous skills/knowledge needed

No previous skills are essential, but some experience of or knowledge of 'rap' rhythms would be helpful.

Key background information

It is a teacher's responsibility to introduce children to a wide range of authors and to different styles of literature, including humour and fantasy. Bear in mind also that short poems are ideal for younger children as they can quickly absorb them by heart, which aids their reading skills as well as boosting their confidence.

This activity involves work at text level and also at word level for some.

Preparation

Copy onto a large sheet of paper or OHT the humorous title poem from Brian Moses's collection *Hippopotamus Dancing* (Cambridge University Press) which is reproduced as photocopiable sheets 109 and 110.

Practise reading it aloud to get the hang of the rap rhythm, so that you can give a convincing performance in class. The better you know the poem, the less reliant on the written text you will be, hence the more direct interaction you can have with the audience of children.

Resources needed

Maracas, Indian bells, wooden claves, guiros (any instruments that can be played easily in the hands), a copy

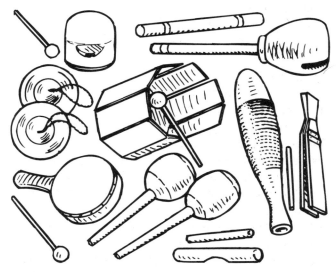

of the poem 'Hippopotamus dancing', a flip chart, board or OHP, art and writing materials, copies of photocopiable sheets 109 and 110 for children needing support.

What to do

Tell the children that they are going to learn another poem to add to their growing repertoire today – about hippos! Ask if any of them have ever seen any hippos, perhaps on a visit with their family to a zoo or a safari park. Some children may have been on a package holiday to Africa and seen hippos in the wild. Others may have watched nature programmes on television. All may remember books read in school, such as *Hot Hippo* by Mwenye Hadithi (Knight Books), or may have browsed through information books about hippos in the school or local library. Encourage the children to recount their experiences and to tell you all they know about hippos.

Then ask the class if any of them have ever seen or heard of hippos dancing – if not, why not? Let them know that they are in for a big surprise, and read the 'Hippopotamus dancing' poem, accentuating the rhythms. Encourage the children to read the poem with you, then once more while clapping the beat. Next, you could recite it in two parts, with half of the class saying lines 1 and 3 and the other half lines 2 and 4, and so on, or ring the changes by repeating the last two lines before the refrain for each verse. You could also invite the children to work out an alternative refrain that would keep the same rhythm, and round off the session by dancing about the room while reciting the poem!

As a follow-up activity, the children could organize a hippos' boogie ball, which would involve drawing up a guest list, designing invitation cards and luxurious dresses and suits for the hippo guests. You could describe the arrival of the VIP hippos for the local newspaper, interviewing some of the most important guests, write menus for the buffet supper, and songs for the entertainers.

Some children might like to research factual information about hippopotami.

Suggestion(s) for extension

Children could make a collection of humorous poems about animals. They could hunt for other poems that include a refrain, choose one and practise performing it to show in an assembly.

Suggestion(s) for support

Give out photocopiable sheets 109 and 110 to children who need further practice to develop their phonological skills. Ask them to underline the pairs of rhyming words. They could also be asked in another session to generate lists of words with the same spelling pattern as words in the poem – *oo* (boogaloo), or the same initial sound, *sh* (shuffle), *tr* (trot), *fl* (flab).

Assessment opportunities

Monitor the children's reading skills as they read the poem aloud; note how quickly they commit the poem to memory; note their ability to clap to the rhythm.

Opportunities for IT

Children could practise keyboard skills by using the computer to transcribe their follow-up work. They could create a database of the words they generate with the same spelling patterns.

Display ideas

Large paintings of the hippos dancing could be produced to be displayed alongside an enlarged version of the poem. Children's accounts of real experiences of hippos at safari parks or on holiday abroad could also be displayed. Half the class could present a choral reading in a school assembly, while others perform the hippos' dance and supply music to accompany the refrain.

Other aspects of the English PoS covered

Speaking and listening – 1a, c; 2b.
Writing – 1b, c; 2a, c, d, e; 3b.

Reference to photocopiable sheets

The poem 'Hippopotamus dancing' is reproduced on photocopiable sheets 109 and 110. Some children will use it to help their phonological skills. They will be expected to underline rhyming words and to focus on specific spelling patterns in words used in the text.

Hippopotamus dancing (cont.)

Hip-hippo, hippopotamus dancing,
Hip-hippo, hippopotamus dancing.

Hippos in tutus,
hippos in vests,
baby hippos
doing their best
to keep clear of Dad
as he stumbles around,
causing commotion,
shaking the ground.

Hip-hippo, hippopotamus dancing,
Hip-hippo, hippopotamus dancing.

Brian Moses

LISTEN, LEARN AND THINK!

For the children to: extend rhyming patterns by analogy, generating new words; discriminate onsets and rimes.

†† *Oral session: whole class. Children working in groups. Feedback session: whole class.*

⏱ *Oral session: 20–25 minutes. Group work session: 15–20 minutes. Feedback session: 10–15 minutes.*

Previous skills/knowledge needed.

The children should be able to recognize pairs of words that rhyme and have had experience of supplying words that rhyme with given words. An acquaintance with the terms 'onset' and 'rime' would also be helpful.

Key background information

This session further reinforces development of language awareness, and the ability to supply rhyming words by analogy with known ones, by changing the 'onset' and keeping the same 'rime'. Understanding that you can have different visual spelling patterns for the same rhyming sound is a further milestone in language awareness. Ideally, this work should be carried out within the context of other classroom activities on dinosaurs, to provide a meaningful experience for the children.

Whole to part phonics: how children learn to read and spell by Henrietta Dombey, et al (Centre for Language in Primary Education) is full of valuable information and teaching ideas to support word level work, for instance for the National Literacy Hour.

Preparation

Get to know the poem 'Trouble at the Dinosaur Café' by Brian Moses on photocopiable sheets 111 and 112 yourself by reading it aloud several times before the session. If you decide to use the story *Long Neck and Thunderfoot* in this activity familiarize yourself with the characters beforehand.

Resources needed

A copy of *Long Neck and Thunderfoot* by Helen Piers with illustrations by Michael Foreman (Picture Puffin) (optional), photocopiable sheets 111 and 112, a copy of photocopiable sheet 113 for each child, a flip chart, writing materials.

What to do

Ask the children to recap on what they already know about dinosaurs: for instance the different categories (vegetarian and meat-eaters; residents of land, water, air; armoured and non-armoured, and so on); names and their origins; descriptions of size, shape, weight, skin texture. If you wish, read the story *Long Neck and Thunderfoot* by Helen Piers and discuss the anxieties of the two main characters. Tell the children that you are now going to read a poem called 'Trouble at the Dinosaur Café' by Brian Moses. Ask them if they can guess from the title what sort of trouble it might be.

Read the poem with accentuated expression, pausing before the last word of the last line of each verse to allow the children to supply the rhyming word, and make the most of the last few scary words!

Organize the children into groups and give out copies of photocopiable sheet 113 which asks the children to

make lists of words that rhyme with the words on the sheet taken from the poem: fine, pie, gulp, eat, day, chair, stew.

Have a brief brainstorming burst to get the children started. Draw their attention to the fact that you can take away the first sound, the onset of a word, and go through the alphabet adding a different sound to the rime, the bit that's left, to create a new rhyming word, st/*ew* – br/*ew* – ch/*ew*. You could also mention that sometimes you get differences in spelling of the rhyming pairs in the poem: st*ew* and *you* / p*ie* and *eye* / ch*air* and st*are*.

When the children have finished compiling their lists, gather together to share their findings. Write some of their rhyming words on the flip chart.

Suggestion(s) for extension
Confident children could prepare a choral reading of the poem, paying particular attention to the voice required to interpret the personality of Tyrannosaurus Rex.

Suggestion(s) for support
When working with photocopiable sheet 113, some children will rely heavily on the sound of the rimes and will be less ready to take on board the differences in spelling. Adult support will be essential for them, but do not expect too much too soon.

Assessment opportunities
Children's ability to provide the missing rhyme as you read will be indicative of their progress in phonological awareness. Progress in differentiating onset and rime can be monitored in the task of supplying a list of rhyming words.

Opportunities for IT
More experienced computer users could experiment with tabs and columns to store their word collections.

Display ideas
You could create a wall display of a 'dinosaur dynasty'. Poems about dinosaurs, written out neatly, could provide panels.

Other aspects of the English PoS covered
Speaking and listening – 1a, c; 2b; 3b.
Writing – 3b.

Reference to photocopiable sheets
Photocopiable sheets 111 and 112 reproduce the poem 'Trouble at the Dinosaur Café' on which this activity is based.

Photocopiable sheet 113 provides children with an opportunity to generate lists of rhyming words by making analogies with given words. It will help to reinforce discrimination of onset and rime.

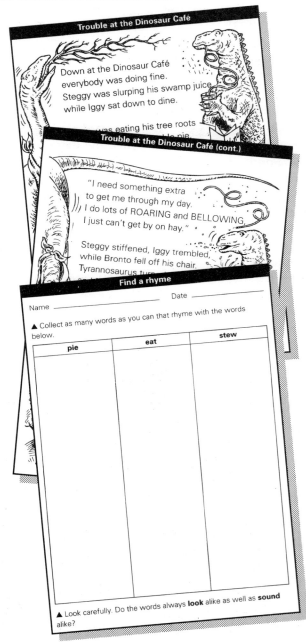

Trouble at the Dinosaur Café

Down at the Dinosaur Café everybody was doing fine. Steggy was slurping his swamp juice while Iggy sat down to dine.

...was eating his tree roots

Trouble at the Dinosaur Café (cont.)

"I need something extra to get me through my day. I do lots of ROARING and BELLOWING, I just can't get by on hay."

Steggy stiffened, Iggy trembled, while Bronto fell off his chair. Tyrannosaurus tur...

Find a rhyme

Name _____ Date _____

▲ Collect as many words as you can that rhyme with the words below.

pie	eat	stew

▲ Look carefully. Do the words always **look** alike as well as **sound** alike?

CREATING A CLASS ANTHOLOGY

For the children to: extend their experience of poetry by collecting favourite poems for a class anthology; identify and discuss favourite poems and poets, using appropriate terms – poet, poem, verse, rhyme, rhythm; recognize when reading aloud is effective; participate in reading poems aloud; show good presentational skills when reading aloud.

†† *Introductory session: whole class. Children working on their own or in pairs. Feedback and discussion session: whole class. Writing session: children working on their own.*

🕐 *Introductory session: 15 minutes. Individual/pair work session: 10 minutes. Feedback and discussion session: 20–25 minutes. Writing session: 15 minutes.*

Previous skills/knowledge needed
Children should have encountered anthologies of poetry, preferably with a range of different selection criteria.

Key background information
Book-making has been recognized as an integral part of encouraging children to become readers and writers – see Paul Johnson's books, *Children Making Books* (RALIC) and *A Book of One's Own* (Hodder and Stoughton), if you still need convincing! Understanding the needs of a reader is a crucial ingredient for becoming a writer.

Preparation
Assemble a varied collection of poetry anthologies to share with the class, such as *All join In!* by Quentin Blake (Red Fox); *Early Years Poems and Rhymes* compiled by Jill Bennett (Scholastic); *Commotion in the Ocean* and *Rumble in the Jungle* by Giles Andreae and David Wojtowycz (Orchard); *Lollipop* books, such as *Bouncing Ben and other rhymes* by John Foster (Oxford University Press). You will find *A guide to Poetry 0–13*, edited by Chris Powling and Morag Styles (Books for Keeps and RALIC), a most useful source of ideas.

Resources needed
A collection of poetry anthologies, book-making and writing materials, access to a computer, a flip chart, a copy of photocopiable sheet 114 for each child.

What to do
As a whole class, explore the published anthologies you have collected. Discuss authors, illustrators, subject matter, style and tone. Ask the children which features of which poems particularly appeal to them and why – being able to join in, enjoying repetitive phrases, the security of a refrain, the musicality of the language (alliteration, assonance, onomatopoeia), anticipating the rhymes, feeling the rhythms, coming across new and unusual words, the content, and so on.

Tell the children that they are going to make a class anthology of their favourite poems. Discuss whether they want a variety of subjects or a common theme, a mixture of styles and tone – humorous, thoughtful, sad – poems that rhyme or don't rhyme, poems that have a repetitive refrain or a sustained rhythm. Write some of their ideas on the flip chart. Once these decisions have been made, children can hunt alone or in pairs to find their favourite poem to be included in the class anthology. Explain that when you regroup to share their choices, they will be

will need the support of an experienced peer or an adult helper when working on the computer.

Assessment opportunities
Note children's knowledge about poets, and their confidence and independence in making choices. Handwriting and/or word-processing expertise and attention to detail in presentation will also be evident, as well as pride in one's work. Fluency and expression when reading aloud should also be noted.

Opportunities for IT
This activity is ideal for creating and editing poems and the anthology using DTP.

Display ideas
The anthology should be proudly displayed on the class library bookshelf, after presentation to other classes in a school assembly. Individual poems could be enlarged for display as poem of the week, with a résumé as to why it is a special favourite.

Other aspects of the English PoS covered
Speaking and listening – 1a; 2a.
Writing – 2e.

Reference to photocopiable sheet
Photocopiable sheet 114 offers a framework to prompt children's responses to poetry and to specific features of language use.

expected to say exactly what they like about their chosen poem, why they chose it and how they came to know this poem – perhaps it is a new find, or an old favourite learned in school, or one heard on television or radio, or an old family favourite learned at home. Give a copy of photocopiable sheet 114 as a prompt for their thinking.

After you have regrouped and the children have accounted for their choices, discuss the format the children would prefer for the class book – size, shape, colour of pages, whether to write by hand, word-process or have a mixture of the two, whether to have decorative borders and illustrations, which materials to use for the covers, whether to leave space for blurb and information about the 'editors'.

Now, ask the children to write out their poem neatly or use IT, as preferred. Allot short sessions during the week to create attractive covers, blurb, and so on, and to assemble the book.

Suggestion(s) for extension
Children could prepare a taped version of the anthology for the class listening corner, with each child reading their own choice onto the tape, after careful rehearsal and discussion about the qualities that contribute towards a successful reading, such as speed of delivery, volume, intonation, emphasis, pauses.

Suggestion(s) for support
Some children lack confidence in making choices, and an adult partner would be a great help to ask supportive questions, jog the memory and praise ideas. Some children

My favourite poem

Name _____ Date _____

Poem: _____

I like this poem because _____

My favourite part is _____

Here are the words/phrases that I like best: _____

I know some other poems by the same writer: _____

I know some other poems on the same theme: _____

CRITICS' CORNER

For the children to: discuss poems read; compare and contrast themes in poems; comment on patterns of sound, word combinations and forms of presentation; discuss meanings of words and phrases that create humour and sound effects in poetry.

†† *Introductory session: whole class. Writing session: children working individually or in pairs. Feedback session: whole class.*

🕐 *Introductory session: 20 minutes. Writing session: 20–25 minutes. Feedback session: 10–15 minutes.*

Previous skills/knowledge needed
Children will need to have been introduced to a variety of poems and poets. It would be helpful if they knew a few poems by heart, and if the class had already undertaken the work in 'Creating a class anthology'.

Key background information
Once children are familiar with a variety of poets and have a growing repertoire of poems known by heart, it is appropriate to extend their thinking and encourage them to talk about poetic features – sound effects, such as rhyme, rhythm, alliteration; meanings, as in word choices and word combinations, similes, metaphors; humorous effects, and so on. This activity provides an opportunity for focused work at text, sentence and word level.

Preparation
Collect reviews of poetry from newspapers, local and national, and magazines, such as *Carousel, Books for Keeps, The School Librarian.*

Resources needed
A collection of poetry reviews, a flip chart, writing paper and writing materials.

What to do
Show the children your collection of reviews from the press and read one or two examples about books of poetry, preferably about poets they are familiar with. Tell them how important it is for you as a teacher to have critics' views to help to find out what new books have been published and which ones are thought to be worthwhile, and to help you choose which books to buy for the school library.

Tell the children that they are going to be critics for the day – and hopefully for life! Note the features that the established critics comment on – subject matter, feelings and meanings, language use, the impact on the reader. Share together some ideas about a poem that you have read together recently, and brainstorm on the flip chart the features the children believe to be worth commenting on – remind them of the features you had discussed earlier when creating your class anthology.

Suggest that the children now work alone or in pairs to write a review of a favourite poem – perhaps the one they chose for the class anthology – modelling their review on the pattern just shared with the whole class.

When the work has been completed, gather as a whole class again and ask some children to read their reviews to the group. Encourage the other children to add comments and to express their appreciation of their friends' efforts.

As a follow-up activity, children might like to send their reviews to the publisher or to the poet, if he or she is still alive. They will need to compose a covering letter too, which could include how the children first came across this particular poem and/or other works by the same poet. They might also like to enquire about future publications that are in the pipeline.

Suggestion(s) for extension

You could set competent children a specific task of hunting for similes or checking any new vocabulary in a dictionary. They could also compose a poem on the same subject, or with a similar rhythmical pattern or repetitive refrain.

Suggestion(s) for support

Some children may need to work in a more supportive situation with a friend and produce a joint review. Pair work lends a feeling of security to many young learners.

Assessment opportunities

Note children's use of correct terminology when discussing their poems and their awareness of poetic features. There are also opportunities to monitor growing independence as writers and the development of writing skills, such as spelling, punctuation and handwriting.

Opportunities for IT

Children could use the computer to format a magazine style page layout (as in *Books for Keeps* that you may have shown them at the start of the session) to present their reviews.

Display ideas

Build a 'Critics' corner' in your classroom to display reviews that children can add to over time. You could make space for any replies the children might receive from publishers or poets.

Other aspects of the English PoS covered

Speaking and listening – 1a, c; 2a, b; 3b.
Writing – 1a, b, c; 2b, c, d, e; 3a, b.

POETRY FESTIVAL

For the children to: be introduced to poems by significant children's authors; be introduced to poems from a range of cultures; practise reading aloud to an audience.

†† *Introductory session: whole class. Reading sessions: whole class.*

🕐 *Introductory session: 20 minutes. Reading sessions: 5–10 minutes each.*

Previous skills/knowledge needed

Children should understand the role of an author and have had experience of talking about poems and justifying their choices of favourites.

Key background information

Familiarity with poems and stories breeds confidence and enjoyment for young children, so the better they know their authors, the more fun they will have and the more discerning they will become. They deserve to get to know the best available, where language is used with flair and imagination. The suggestions in this section could easily be incorporated into Literacy Hour activities at text level.

Preparation

Make a collection of books by acclaimed poets from a range of cultures, such as Michael Rosen, John Agard, Grace Nichols, Allan Arlberg, Roger McGough, Brian Patten, Kit Wright. Mount an attractive display in the classroom.

Resources needed

Books from the display, tape recorder and cassettes, a flip chart, writing materials.

What to do

Introduce the children to your project for this half-term – to celebrate the best of children's poetry in a class poetry festival. Ask the children for their current favourite contenders to be included in the festival and make a list of them on a flip chart sheet to be kept on display during the festival. Then share a few of the books you have already

assembled on display. Suggest that you get to know a 'poet of the week', one by one, by reading from their body of work every day that week at the start of the school day, after play, before dinner, at the start of the afternoon session. Let the children vote on their choice for the first 'poet of the week' to begin proceedings.

Read one of the poems, perhaps one that the children already know well, and encourage them to join in with your reading. Then introduce a new one and read it to the children. Ask them to comment on it afterwards, perhaps prompting them to mention the important features that impact on the reader, such as rhythm, alliteration, onomatopoeia, rhyme, similes, metaphors, word choices and layout. You could round off the session by suggesting that the children prepare a two-part choral reading, with half the class reading alternate verses, to be taped later in the week and added to the stock in the listening corner. Time will need to be set aside for this.

Throughout the week, read new poems by the same author and keep revisiting familiar ones too. You could put the name of the 'poet of the week' on a fresh flip chart sheet each week and list the titles of the poems that have been read each day as a reminder. Encourage children to prepare readings of their favourite one to read aloud to an audience, in the school assembly at the end of the week.

Suggestion(s) for extension
Children could write a review of their favourite poem by the 'poet of the week' to read out in assembly when they present the poem to the school.

Suggestion(s) for support
For a choral reading, some children may be helped by having an adult partner to ensure that they read with expression, clearly and audibly.

Assessment opportunities
Note children's willingness to express their opinions in a whole-class situation, and their oral presentational skills when they read to the larger whole school audience in assembly.

Display ideas
Keep board or wall space free to mount a changing weekly display throughout the festival to highlight the 'poet of the week', including the list of poems by the poet read during the week. Posters could be obtained from bookshops and publishers. Children could do paintings or drawings of the poet; favourite poems could be word-processed or hand-written, with reviews posted alongside; or they could write poems on a same theme.

Other aspects of the English PoS covered
Speaking and listening – 1a, c; 2b; 3b.
Writing – 2b, e.

ALL JOIN IN!

For the children to: learn and recite a new poem; extend a poem following the rhythm of the original; discriminate syllables in words; develop phonological awareness and identify initial sounds.

†† *Oral session: whole class. Children working in pairs. Final session: whole class.*

🕐 *Oral session: 20 minutes. Pair work session: 10–15 minutes. Final session: 10–15 minutes.*

Previous skills /knowledge needed
Children will need to have experience of clapping syllabic rhythms when reciting poems or singing songs. Familiarity with the term 'syllable' and some experience of counting them as they clap out words would also be helpful.

Key background information
Joining in and being caught up with the rhythm and flow of choral reading of poetry plays an important role for young literacy learners. This enjoyment can be followed by some detailed attention at word level, so that the children move from whole to part and not vice versa.

Preparation
You will need a copy of the Big Book version of *Really Rapt* by Susan Hill (Heinemann). You might like to invest in a stand to support Big Books while you are reading from them, as they are increasingly being featured in packages of reading materials.

Resources needed
A copy of *Really Rapt*, writing materials, a flip chart or board, a copy of photocopiable sheet 115 for each child.

What to do
If possible, use the Big Book version of *Really Rapt* so that the whole class will be able to see the print easily. Read the poem 'Chicken and chips', pointing to the words as you read along the lines, orally accentuating the rhythm and the sound patterns. Encourage the children to join in

children to count out the syllables by tapping them out with the fingers of one hand.

Suggestion(s) for support

Some children may need adult support to help them recognize syllables. Clapping, counting and marking off syllables will also help.

Assessment opportunities

Monitor children's ease in learning the poem and reciting it with expression. You can also note their growing ability to keep the beat and the full syllabic rhythm when they clap. Check also their accuracy in counting syllables and in supplying other words with the required number of syllables.

Display ideas

A quick display of 'work in progress' could show the lists of words the children have come up with. Some children could make 3-D plates of food to go with the poem, and they could invent recipes for these and draw up menus for special occasions.

Other aspects of the English PoS covered

Speaking and listening –1a; 2a; 3b.
Writing – 3b.

Reference to photocopiable sheet

Photocopiable sheet 115 requires children to discriminate between words of differing numbers of syllables and to generate further words by matching the number of syllables.

with you as soon as they pick up the repetitive refrain. Read it once more with everyone joining in as best they can. Now ask the children for further suggestions for extra verses to the poem, to include combinations of foods they would enjoy or that they would find amusing. Of course they have to keep to the established rhythm of the poem. Children usually come up with all sorts of exuberant combinations, such as 'jelly and chips', 'strawberries and chips', 'chocolate bars and chips'.

You could add variations, such as clapping the beat, finger clicking, foot tapping, swaying. You could move on to clapping the full syllabic rhythm. You might also like to try a two-part reading, with half the class reciting the lead lines and half the refrain.

Set the children off in pairs with copies of photocopiable sheet 115 to find the words from the poem with one, two, three and four syllables and to generate as many more words as they can to fill the sheet. Finally, gather as a class to share lists. To reinforce the learning point, you could scribe a selection of words on the flip chart, marking off the syllables and clapping them together.

To develop general phonological awareness, you could use words from this poem in follow-up activities. For instance, children could be asked to make a collection of all the words they know beginning with *ch*, to include proper nouns, common nouns, adjectives, adverbs, verbs. They could generate alliterative sentences based on *ch*. They could write a story that has to have one *ch* word per sentence.

Some children might like to begin compiling a database on the computer that they can keep adding to in the future. They could recite other poems in the book, for instance, 'Wobbly Wheel' and go on to explore word level work on *w/wh*.

Suggestion(s) for extension

Children could extend their experience with syllables by writing Haiku, the Japanese 'snapshot' form of poetry consisting of only three lines, where the first line has five syllables, the second seven and the third five. Encourage

---

How many syllables?

Name _____ Date _____

▲ Hunt for words with the same number of syllables as the words below. Add any more of your own that you think of.

chips (1)	chicken (2)	everyone (3)

Can you find any words with 4 syllables?

VISITING POET

For the children to: become well-acquainted with the work of one poet; read a range of different text types with confidence.

†† *Oral session: whole class. Writing sessions: children working alone, in pairs or small groups. Feedback session: whole class.*

🕐 *Oral session: 20 minutes. Writing sessions: 30–35 minutes each. Feedback sessions: 20 minutes each.*

Previous skills /knowledge needed

Children should be well acquainted with the work of the poets shortlisted for the visit, and be confident in asking questions and talking about their response to poems.

Key background information

It is well documented that meeting real authors and being involved in working with them in school makes a tremendous impact on both the enthusiasm and the confidence of young readers and writers. Seeing for themselves how established poets set about their writing, create effects for their readers, provide them with important clues to meanings, draw them into the story with illustrations and captivate their audience with expressive readings leads to a growth in children's skills, both as readers and writers.

Here the focus is on text-level learning.

Preparation

You will need to do some preliminary research into poets who are prepared to visit schools. *Looking for an author* compiled by the Book Trust and RALIC, and published by RALIC is a very useful booklet. It details the availability of writers, the age and size of group they are prepared to work with, the sort of activities they will engage in and, last but not least, the costs involved.

Make a preliminary shortlist of three possibilities before involving the class in the final decision. Collect copies of the works of the poets on your shortlist. Once the visit is booked, gather together a full collection of the works of the poet who has agreed to undertake the visit, plus any publicity posters from the publishers to whet the children's appetite.

Resources needed

Copies of the work of the poets on your shortlist, a flip chart or board, writing paper, drawing and writing materials, access to a computer, copies of photocopiable sheet 116 for those children involved in creating the display board for the visiting poet.

What to do

Tell the class that you are going to invite a poet to come to school to work with them. Explain to the children that writers are very busy people and that they will need to arrange the poets in order of preference, in case their first choice is not available. Show them the shortlist of the three names on the flip chart, all of whom the children should be familiar with and have enjoyed reading in the recent past. Revisit a selection of the poets' work to refresh their memories, and involve the children themselves in the readings. Talk about the pros and cons for each one, before asking the children to vote on their order of preference.

Together, make a list of all the jobs that need to be done to organize the visit – fix a date, write a letter of invitation, send a letter to parents, a welcome poster, display books and work carried out by the children in connection with the chosen author, prepare a list of questions to ask the poet and reviews of the poet's work to share with her/him, write a welcome speech, a thank-you speech and a thank-you letter.

Organize the children to carry out all these tasks, allowing plenty of time to ensure effective results, possibly several sessions. Some children may be confident and able enough to work alone, others can work in pairs or small groups, according to their experience and/or need for support. One group could use photocopiable sheet 116 to help them plan and design a display board to celebrate the work of the visiting poet.

Suggestion(s) for extension
Children could give a running report on the progress of the arrangements in a five-minute slot in one of the school assemblies each week.

Suggestion(s) for support
Mixed-ability pairing or grouping will offer the support needed to less experienced children, as would adult co-operation on the computer, when drafting letters and speeches.

Assessment opportunities
Throughout, you could monitor children's listening and responding skills, their confidence and fluency when putting their suggestions orally to the group, their cueing strategies when reading, their performance skills when reading aloud, their planning and writing skills and their fluency and accuracy when reading back their own writing. You could also note more experienced children's skills in supporting their peers in a helpful and sensitive manner when working in mixed-ability groupings.

Opportunities for IT
Clearly there is a wealth of opportunities here, as most of the writing tasks could be carried out on the computer to provide a professional finish. You need to ensure that everyone has a fair share of operating the keyboard when children are working in small groups.

Display ideas
Gradually build up a whole wall display round the collection of the poet's works: a step-by-step description of the planning stages and how the visit came to fruition; an account of the actual visit itself with photos, drawings and paintings; personal comments on the visit from the children, staff and parents involved; copies of subsequent letters and any poems that the children produced as a result of the visit.

Other aspects of the English PoS covered
Speaking and listening – 1a, c; 2a, b.
Writing – 1a, b, c; 2b, c, d, e; 3a.

Reference to photocopiable sheet
Photocopiable sheet 116 offers the opportunity for children to plan in advance the design for display with appropriate eye-catching headings.

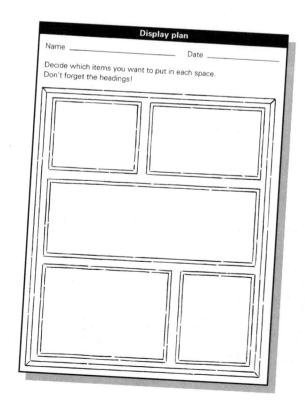

ANYTHING THEY CAN DO...

For the children to: use humorous verse as a structure to write their own poems by adaptation, mimicry or substitution.

†† *Oral session: whole class. Writing session: working alone or in pairs. Feedback session: whole class.*

⏲ *Oral session: 15 minutes. Writing session: 20 minutes. Feedback session: 15 minutes.*

Previous skills/knowledge needed

Children will need to know by heart the traditional rhyme 'Monday's child is fair of face'.

Key background information

Starting from a secure base with a poem that is already very familiar to children lends a great deal of security to young readers and writers. They can be assured of success by modelling their own work on the structured framework of the original. As always, publishing children's work does wonders for their self-image.

Preparation

Make an enlarged copy or OHT of photocopiable sheet 117 for use in the whole-class session.

Resources needed

A copy of *Catch Them If You Can*, an anthology of poems selected by Helen Cook and Morag Styles (Cambridge Univerisity Press), photocopiable sheet 117, a flip chart, board or OHP, writing materials, a copy of photocopiable sheet 118 for each child.

What to do

Ask the children to recite with you the traditional rhyme 'Monday's child is fair of face'. Talk to them about the characteristics of children born on the various days of the week. Do they think the rhyme is true or false? See if they know on which day they were born and check the rhyme against their own personality.

Now read a humorous alternative by Colin McNaughton, 'Monday's child is red and spotty' (from photocopiable page 117). Allow the children to respond spontaneously to this version.

Working with the enlarged copy of the poem displayed for the children to see, read the poem as a class. Together, air a few ideas about how you could change this poem again, for instance by replacing the adjectives with other humorous ones:

Monday's child is big and sporty,
Tuesday's child is very naughty.
Wednesday's child won't go to bed,
Thursday's child is a pain in the head,
and so on.

Hand out copies of photocopiable sheet 118 to each child. Tell the children that they are going to work in pairs or on their own, as they prefer, and write their own humorous version of this rhyming poem. Explain that they can change just the last word in the line or more than that if they wish; they can change both the rhymes at the end of the couplets (make sure they know about couplets) or keep one and change the other, as they prefer. Encourage them to use their imagination to think of various alternatives, and to think hard about their choices of words.

When they have completed the activity, call the class together to share some of the new poems.

Suggestion(s) for extension

Competent children could use the structure of a well-known song to write one of their own. For instance you could teach the children 'What shall we do with a drunken sailor', then sing the Allan Ahlberg rendering of 'What shall we do with a grumpy teacher?' based on the same tune, from *Heard it in the Playground* (Puffin). The familiar tune, the rhythmical pattern and the repetitive refrain will help the children to quickly commit the poem to memory – and the idea of poking fun at teachers guarantees this will be a great hit with children! They could then add more verses themselves.

You could move some children on to read some nonsense verse, where poets indulge in the pure pleasure of playing with language and zany ideas, drawing on the work of Edward Lear, Lewis Carroll and Spike Milligan, for instance. Others might like to write their own version of 'Pet Food', from *Catch Them If You Can*.

There are plenty of opportunities for this sort of modelling: 'Great Day' by Michael Rosen (*You Wait Till I'm Older Than You*, Puffin) has proved very popular with Key Stage 1 classes, as most children feel they, too, have days that are just like this!

Suggestion(s) for support

Some children will need to tackle this activity as a shared writing experience, working in a small group with an adult as scribe and prompter, instead of on their own.

A few children may need to build confidence by modelling the basic structure from a very well-known song, such as 'Here we go round the mulberry bush' instead of a poem – everyday actions usually spring readily to children's minds, however inexperienced they are.

Assessment opportunities

You can assess children's skill in using a set framework as a model for their own writing. General writing skills, such as spelling, punctuation and handwriting can also be monitored.

Opportunities for IT

The computer can be used for composing writing, from the planning stages right through to 'publication'.

Display ideas

You could display all the children's versions of poems alongside Colin McNaughton's and the traditional version. They could add their comments about the old-fashioned view of children in the traditional rhyme. As encouragement to other budding poets, ask them to write down how they worked from the model to produce their own poem.

A song writers' corner could be set up, where all the new songs could be displayed, with taped versions on hand to listen to and sing along with.

Other aspects of the English PoS covered

Speaking and listening – 1a, c; 2b.
Writing – 1b, c; 2b, c, d, e; 3b.

Reference to photocopiable sheets

Photocopiable sheet 117 is provided to enlarge and use in the whole class introductory session.

Photocopiable sheet 118 requires children to complete a poem, based on a well-known structure, in their own way, bearing in mind the rhythmical and rhyming patterns.

Monday's child is red and spotty

Monday's child is red and spotty,
Tuesday's child won't use the potty.
Wednesday's child won't go to bed.
Thursday's child will not be fed.
Friday's child breaks all his toys,
Saturday's child makes an awful noise.
And the child that's born on the seventh day
Is a pain in the neck like the rest, OK!

Colin McNaughton

Monday's child is...

Name _____ Date _____

Here is your chance to create a new poem.
▲ Share some ideas with a friend before you write.

Monday's child is _____
Tuesday's child is _____
Wednesday's child is _____
Thursday's child is _____
Friday's child is _____
Saturday's child is _____
But the child that is born on the Sabbath day
Is _____

LISTEN AND WRITE

For the children to: select words with care, re-reading and listening for effect; use similes and alternative words and phrases to express meaning.

†† *Listening and oral session: whole class. Writing session: individual or whole class.*

⏱ *Listening and oral session: 35–40 minutes for inexperienced classes. Writing session: 30–40 minutes.*

Previous skills/knowledge needed

It would be preferable if children had already had experience of keeping a poetry jotter. Some familiarity with similes would also be useful.

Key background information

Listening skills are vital for literacy development, as is the skill of imaging in the mind. Constructing pictures from the written word is the starting point for developing higher order reading skills that go beyond the literal. Children need plenty of practice to develop such skills. They also need to experience several shared writing sessions to build their confidence and skill in composing poems, and to be shown how to move into poetic form from initial ideas in note and prose form. From a young age children should be encouraged to keep a poetry jotter at the ready to write down or draw ideas as they occur.

The focus in this activity is largely at text level.

Preparation

Record shortish excerpts from a range of different types of music – classical, pop, reggae, Chinese, South American, Indian, for example. Choose fairly accessible pieces, including one of your own favourites, that will have an immediate appeal for young children and will be relatively easy to interpret.

Resources needed

Tape recorder, tapes of selected music and blank cassettes, a flip chart, writing and drawing materials, a poetry jotter for each child.

What to do

Explain to the class that this is going to be a special week because you are going to spend time each day listening in silence to different types of music. Start with a piece that you yourself are very fond of and follow the same pattern for the listening sessions throughout the week. Tell the children that they can listen with their eyes closed if that helps them to concentrate. Ask them to focus on what they feel, and the pictures that come into their heads as they listen to the music. Keep the listening time reasonably short so as not to make too many demands on the children, if they are unused to this type of activity.

When the music has ended, talk to the class first of all about whether they enjoyed the music, and about any memories that the music brought back to them. Most of us need more than one hearing to finalize our responses, so listen once more to the recording. This time as the

children listen, encourage them to jot down notes and/or drawings in their poetry jotter about the scenes that spring to mind or the feelings that are aroused – sad, happy, funny, frightened, lonely, mischievous, and so on. At the end, they can share their jottings and you could scribe their thoughts on the flip chart to compare the children's different interpretations. Keep these flip-chart notes for the children to refer to later, when they work on their poems individually. When the children begin composing their poems, remind them to search for expressive vocabulary and to try to include some similes.

Some children will be helped by having more individual attention, working one to one with an adult to talk through their impressions in more detail and to organize their thoughts more clearly. Others, with less well developed writing skills, will benefit from individual help when committing their thoughts to paper by hand or on a computer. If the class is inexperienced at writing poems, then focus on one of the ideas supplied by the children during the listening sessions and create a poem as a shared piece of writing, using this framework:

▲ Write about the most interesting parts from the list.

▲ Write the ideas out in full sentences composed by the children, making decisions as you go by asking them questions and taking a vote if disagreements arise about wording or emphasis.

▲ When you have finished, ask the children why the text they have created is not yet a poem.

▲ Dispose of any redundant words and lay out the text in a different format.

▲ As you change things, check for ways of improving vocabulary, punctuation and so on.

▲ Keep reading the words aloud to hear how the poem sounds – this is a very useful tool for helping poets to make choices.

▲ Write out the finished, agreed version and read the poem aloud together.

(From: *Curriculum Bank Reading Key Stage 1*, page 96)

Suggestion(s) for extension and support

This poetry writing activity allows children with little or no experience to begin writing poetry for themselves, and gives children with some experience an opportunity to extend and develop their skills.

Assessment opportunities

You may notice considerable differences in children's attention spans and the quality of their listening skills. Note also their ability to image in the mind. As they write and read back their work, you can glean valuable information about their development as writers and readers, through their vocabulary choices, attention to layout, oral expression and so on.

Display ideas

A writing workshop table could be provided with a tape recorder and tapes of various pieces of music for children to listen to at their leisure.

Other aspects of the English PoS covered

Speaking and listening – 1a, b; 2a, b.
Writing – 1b, c; 2b, c, d, e; 3b.

LOOK AND WRITE

For the children to: look closely; make inferences and predictions; further develop their understanding of poetic form; read their poems in a familiar setting; prepare and present poems to a larger audience.

†† *Introductory session: whole class. Writing sessions: children working alone, in pairs or small groups. Feedback session: whole class. Reading preparation sessions: children working in pairs.*

🕐 *Introductory session: 15–20 minutes. Writing session: 25–30 minutes. Feedback session: 20 minutes. Reading preparation sessions: 5–10 minutes each.*

Previous skills/knowledge needed
It would be helpful if the children have already spent time in class looking at and talking about illustrations in books. It would also be beneficial if they had already completed the activity 'Listen and write' on page 59.

Key background information
The National Curriculum demands that children are provided with a variety of different stimuli to activate their imagination and lead to further reading and writing opportunities. Children also need time to polish their poetry writing skills and their reading aloud skills.

Preparation
Make a collection of prints, postcards, photographs and books of paintings and drawings, ranging from the Old Masters to the modern, and from countries across the world as well as from Europe, from women as well as male artists. Try to find examples that will stimulate the sort of questions suggested in 'What to do'.

Resources needed
A collection of visual material (as above), a flip chart or board, poetry jotters, drawing and writing materials, a copy of photocopiable sheet 119 for each child.

What to do
If the children have already worked with music as a stimulus for writing poetry (see the previous activity, 'Listen and write', remind them about what they did then. Explain that this week they are going to do something similar, but this week it is their eyes and not their ears that will do the preliminary work! Remind them about book illustrations that you have looked at and discussed in class recently – paying attention to details, searching closely for the clues the illustrator gives us, reading beyond the surface of the picture. Explain that they can apply the same principles to looking at paintings.

Choose one painting and show it to the class. Then draw up a list of questions together, as in the following example, to remind them of how to approach the task: *Who are the people in the painting? Where are they and why are they there? When is the scene taking place? What are the people feeling? Why? What has just happened? What might happen next?* Let the children respond briefly and spontaneously, using the list of questions as a stimulus. Write their comments on the flip chart.

Divide the class to work individually, in pairs or small groups, and explain that they are now going to compose a poem with the same title as the painting. Hand out a copy of photocopiable sheet 119 to each child, as a framework to guide their thinking as they begin the writing activity. Remind the children of the strategies they use to turn their jottings into a poem, as set out in the previous activity in this book (and in *Curriculum Bank Reading Key Stage 1*, page 96, used as a framework for inexperienced poetry writers). Some children may need the help of an adult to promote discussion by reading the prompts from the photocopiable sheet and acting as scribe or secretary at the computer keyboard. This will transform the experience for less advanced readers and writers.

When the task is completed, bring the children together again to read their poems aloud to the class.

As in the listening/poetry-writing activity, continue in this way throughout the week, responding to different paintings/pictures. You could also allow preparation times for children to polish their reading aloud skills in readiness for a poetry reading assembly, which the children's parents could attend.

Suggestion(s) for extension and support
Children at all levels of competence and experience will be able to participate successfully in this activity.

Assessment opportunities
Note children's keenness to 'look with intent', to draw conclusions from the evidence provided by the painter and to move into the realm of the imagination. You will also be able to monitor their writing skills, their reading aloud skills and their general confidence in themselves as readers and writers, as well as their understanding of the characteristics of a poem.

Opportunities for IT
Drawing on children's DTP skills, you could work towards a class publication of 'Poems and paintings' by the end of the week.

Display ideas
You can add the children's poems to the initial display of postcards, prints, art books and the work of established poets.

Other aspects of the English PoS covered
Speaking and listening – 1a, b, c; 2a, b; 3a.
Writing – 1b, c; 2b, c, d, e; 3a, b.

Reference to photocopiable sheet
Photocopiable sheet 119 provides a set of crucial questions as an *aide-mémoire* to support children's written responses to the paintings.

Planning a poem

Name _____ Date _____

▲ Jot down your ideas below before you write your poem.

Who are the people in the painting? _____

Where are they? _____

Why are they there? _____

When is the scene taking place? _____

What are the people feeling? Why? _____

What are they thinking? _____

What has just happened? _____

What might happen next? _____

MEMORIES ARE MADE OF THIS

For the children to: select words with care, re-reading and listening for effect; discuss these effects within a familiar group; read own work with expression to a familiar audience.

†† *Oral sessions: whole class. Shared writing session: whole class. Writing session: children working on their own. Oral sessions: whole class.*

🕐 *Oral sessions: 5 minutes each. Shared writing session: 20–25 minutes. Writing session: 30–40 minutes. Oral sessions: 10–15 minutes each.*

Previous skills/knowledge needed

Experience of open discussion about personal events and feelings would be beneficial. Respect for and careful handling of other people's special things is essential.

Key background information

In *Poetry in the Making* (Faber), Ted Hughes spells out what he sees to be the essential ingredients for a good piece of writing. One of these is the choice of topic, which should be centred on something or somebody the writer cares deeply about. This activity provides the children with the opportunity to write about a very special 'treasure', to draft ideas and to shape them into an effective poem. This writing activity lends itself well to parental involvement. It could also provide Literacy Hour work at text, sentence and word level.

Preparation

Choose carefully a special object of your own to take into the class to show to the children – perhaps something from your own childhood, or something one of your own children treasured. You need to make sure that the children understand the importance of all these 'treasures' for their owners, and that they know how to handle precious objects with the utmost care.

Resources needed

Card to make labels, a flip chart or board, drawing and writing materials, poetry jotters.

What to do

In short sessions over the week, ask each child to bring in a treasured possession to display – perhaps their first toy, a family heirloom, an old photo – anything, however small, that has special significance for them. Each child will have the chance to tell the rest of the class about their treasure and why it is so special to them.

Encourage the children to ask each other relevant questions, such as: *Was it given to you? Who gave it to you? Did you find it? How long have you had it? Does it conjure up a happy or a sad memory? Where do you keep it at home? What do you do with it? Do you have imaginary adventures with it?* Start the ball rolling by telling the children about your own treasure, if they are not forthcoming.

Each child can use some of these points to write a label or caption to go with their treasure as it is added to the display.

On the flip chart or board, jot down the most important points about your own treasure. Ask the children to help you to make careful choices of vocabulary to provide as accurate a description as possible, before moving on to note all the special feelings associated with the treasure, and the memories it provokes. Together shape this into a poem, using the strategies outlined on page 60 (and in *Curriculum Bank Reading Key Stage 1*, page 96).

In a subsequent session, children can work individually to create a poem about their own 'treasure'. If you intend to invite the children's parents to join in this session, then you need to organize this well in advance.

Finally, allow a series of short oral sessions for the children to read aloud their finished poems to the class, and to take feedback on the effects they have created in their writing.

Suggestion(s) for extension

More experienced readers could prepare their poems as a cloze procedure activity for their peers, by omitting every tenth word for them to fill in.

Some children could prepare a taped version of the treasure poems for the listening corner, with some poems being read by individuals, some as choral readings, some read in parts and some accompanied by percussion or body sounds.

Suggestion(s) for support

Working in pairs raises children's confidence. A friend could offer encouragement, but the ideal writing partner in this case would be an adult from the child's family who shares the emotional experience of the child and is familiar with the feelings attached to the special 'treasure'.

Assessment opportunities

There is ample opportunity here to note children's developing listening and response skills, questioning skills, growing vocabulary and confidence in drafting and polishing their writing, as well as their secretarial skills.

Opportunities for IT

With adult support, the class could publish their 'treasure' poems on the word processor, with each child providing an illustration for their own poem. Bilingual children might also like to have their writing translated into their home language.

Display ideas

The display of treasures and captions will grow as the week progresses. Add children's poems as a backcloth to the 3-D display. The published book could take its place on the class library shelf.

Other aspects of the English PoS covered

Speaking and listening – 1a, b, c; 2a, b; 3b.
Writing – 1a, b, c; 2b, c, d, e; 3a, b.

MY FAMILY

For the children to: use speech bubbles correctly; write from personal experience; prepare and present poems to a familiar audience.

†† *Introductory session: whole class. Writing session: children working on their own. Presentation sessions: whole class.*

🕐 *Introductory session: 15–20 minutes. Writing session: 20–25 minutes. Presentation sessions: 15 minutes each.*

Previous skills/knowledge needed

It would be helpful if children had considered the relationship between speech and writing, and if they were familiar with speech and thought bubbles.

Key background information

Michael Rosen in *Did I hear you write?* (André Deutsch) describes how he works very successfully with children, helping to demystify writing for them by getting them to move from everyday oral speech patterns into writing. The main focus in this activity is at text and sentence level.

Preparation

On a flip chart or board, draw your head in profile with speech and thought bubbles in place. Plan what you will write in the session on the flip chart about a special family incident from your life – you can make one up, if you prefer! For instance breakfast time is always chaotic in my house, so I might note 'What I saw' as: 'At top speed, my husband munches his way through his cereal'; 'What I heard' as: 'A batch of mail thuds onto the mat'; 'What I said' as: 'Are you ready for coffee yet?'; and 'What I thought' as: 'Oh, no, I forgot to defrost the bread!'

Resources needed

Prepared plan of incident, A4 sheets of paper, a flip chart or board, writing and drawing materials.

What to do

Begin by telling the children about a special or typical or amusing incident that happened in your family. Working from your prepared plan, tell them that certain aspects have stuck clearly in your mind, that is, you remember clearly what you **said**. Scribe your actual words – be concise, one sentence will suffice – in the speech bubble already drawn on the flip chart. Then tell them that you also remember clearly what you were **thinking**, which was not the same as what you said! Scribe your thoughts in the thought bubble on the chart.

Now turn to what you **saw** with your own eyes, and discuss with the children how to record this on the chart. You could draw a 'sight bubble' from the eyes of the profile, perhaps. Then tell them that you can also recall exactly what you **heard**. Decide with the children's help where to write this – perhaps in a 'hearing bubble' from the ear of the profile.

Read together the sentences that you have written on the flip chart. Ask the children to think about a special family incident that sticks in their mind. Get them to close their eyes and picture an occasion in their family that they remember well. It can be funny, happy, sad, unusual. Ask them to freeze their thoughts at one moment of the incident, and focus on what they saw, heard, said and thought. Share a few of the children's ideas briefly, then give each child an A4 sheet to draw their profile and bubbles and set about the task of writing in: What I said, What I thought, What I saw and What I heard. These sentences will form the basis of their poems.

When everyone has finished, gather as a class for the children to read out their poems and talk about their effects. You will need more than one session for this, so as not to tire the children and have them lose interest in each other's work.

Suggestion(s) for extension

Competent writers could redraft the first versions of their poems, changing words or phrases to improve the effect. They could write out the sentences in a conventional poem format, choosing one of the four items to repeat as a refrain. For instance my breakfast scene might become:

Sam munches away through his cereal stack.
Are you ready for coffee yet?
A batch of mail thuds onto the mat.
Are you ready for coffee yet?
Forgot to defrost the bread last night!
Are you ready for coffee yet?

Confident children could rehearse presentations of their poems for a school assembly, using a range of voices, incorporating sound effects, and so on.

Suggestion(s) for support

Adult prompting to guide thinking about the four categories of comment would raise some children's writing performance. Reminders about vocabulary choices and economy of language for poetry would also be supportive.

Assessment opportunities

Note children's growing competence and confidence when reading together from the flip chart and when reading their own work individually to an audience. During the writing task, you can monitor progress in all areas of writing skills.

Display ideas

A wall of poetry bricks could be mounted under a heading such as 'In Our House'.

Other aspects of the English PoS covered

Speaking and listening – 1a, d; 2a, b.
Writing – 1a, b, c; 2a, c, d, e; 3a.

PET PHRASES

For the children to: engage in a shared reading and writing activity to create a co-operative class poem; prepare and present poems based on familiar settings.

†† *Oral reading and brainstorming session: whole class. Preparation and redrafting sessions: children working on their own then in pairs or small groups.*

🕐 *Oral reading and brainstorming session: 25–30 minutes. Preparation and redrafting sessions: 10–15 minutes each.*

Previous skills/knowledge needed

Children should have had some experience of writing poetry as a shared activity with the support of an adult.

Key background information

Enjoyment and success are two key factors in the learning process. Starting from the known with one's own family provides a guaranteed route to the former, and working with a given structure guarantees the latter. This activity incorporates Literacy Hour work at sentence and text level.

Preparation

Choose one of the following poems about family sayings – or similar ones of your personal choice – to write out onto a flip chart, board or OHT in readiness for a class reading. Prepare to read one of the poems yourself and ask some children to prepare readings of the others.
▲ From *Catch Them If You Can* (Cambridge University Press)
'Never' by eight year old Rebecca Halliday
'Kids' by Spike Milligan
'Don't' by Michael Rosen
▲ From *You Wait Till I'm Older Than You* by Michael Rosen (Puffin)
'Useful Instructions'
▲ From *Hippopotamus Dancing* by Brian Moses (Cambridge University Press)
'My sister said…'

Resources needed

A flip chart, board or OHP, one small piece of paper per child for jotting down a family phrase, writing materials.

What to do

Read one of the poems suggested above, or a similar favourite on the same topic, to the whole class, then in turn ask the children who have prepared readings to read the other three or four. Round off the reading session by asking the whole class to read the poem you have written out in an enlarged format on the flip chart or OHT. Talk with the children about the poems – their basis in family phrases (often from a parent to a child when none too pleased!). Draw attention to any interesting effects such as repetitions and refrains.

Ask the children to think for two minutes in silence and try to come up with a 'pet phrase' from their own family such as, 'Don't you speak to me like that.' 'Would you like to rephrase that, please?' 'Not now Bernard!'

Next, hand out a small piece of paper to each child and ask them to write down their phrase so they don't forget it. Provide individual help if necessary. When all are ready, ask the children in turn, and in quick succession, to read out their phrases. You could repeat the activity starting at the opposite end of the class.

Collect in the pieces of paper and, during the week, transfer the sayings onto a word processor; printing this out as a class poem. Make sufficient copies for one per pair or small group.

Divide the children into pairs or small groups and ask them to read through the poem carefully before 'editing' to give it more shape, more focus, and so on. They could consider altering the order of sayings, repeating some phrases, missing some out, adding more in. You should finish up with several interesting alternative versions.

Suggestion(s) for extension

More confident children could make an audiotape of the different versions for the class listening corner.

Suggestion(s) for support

Inexperienced writers could be asked to focus on one aspect only when improving the class poem, perhaps regrouping phrases or adding a refrain.

Assessment opportunities

Note children's fluency when reading aloud from the displayed text, with the support of the whole class, and when reading aloud their own family phrase to the class. Spelling and grammatical skills will be manifest when children commit their phrase to paper and during redrafting. Note the presentation skills of those children who read an individual poem to the class. Drafting skills can be monitored when children refine the class poem.

Opportunities for IT

The final versions of the class poem could be 'published' using a DTP programme on the computer.

Display ideas

The class could mount a display entitled 'These are a few of our favourite phrases', incorporating the material generated by all the groups; or a poster offering advice to up-and-coming poets in the school.

Other aspects of the English PoS covered

Speaking and listening – 1d; 2b.
Writing – 1a, b, c; 2b; 3a, b.

Non-fiction

Children arrive at school with a wealth of knowledge about print. They will have become aware of the print around them in their local environment and they will probably have had stories read to them face to face, on television or radio programmes, on audiotapes or videos. Some children will also have been taken to their local library and will have found their way to the non-fiction section to browse through books about subjects that interest them – dinosaurs, space, machines and the like. Still, they will almost certainly be much more familiar with the narrative form than with any other.

We need to let children know that reading non-fiction books demands certain similar approaches to reading fiction: for instance we still need a critical reader who will actively engage with the text, who will draw on past experiences, understandings and knowledge in order to comprehend the author's message. But there are also some important differences in the strategies that a reader needs in order to make the most of a non-fiction text as opposed to a narrative one.

Helping children to get into the habit of being researchers in their own right in order to make connections between the known and the new is essential, and yet it has largely been overlooked in schools. Teachers need to offer 'scaffolding' to children to help them avoid copying chunks from a text book wholesale, with little or no understanding; to encourage them to take advantage of the structural features that guide them through a non-fiction text; to enable them to learn a systematic method that will become automatic and stand them in good stead as reading-to-learn researchers throughout their lives.

The following logical steps have been found to be very helpful:
▲ Brainstorm what they know already about the topic.
▲ Establish what they want to know next and formulate a set of questions they want answered.
▲ Locate and select appropriate information.

▲ Evaluate what they find, and adapt their previous thinking in the light of the new information.

Children do not automatically know which questions are appropriate and fruitful to pursue, so teacher modelling is an essential part of the learning process. A simple writing frame format for recording questions, information discovered, and sources used, leads children onto the note-taking procedures of an accomplished researcher. Teachers need also to teach children ways into non-fiction texts via text marking and scanning pages with key-word cards, as well as ways of restructuring new information in a different form.

One important aspect that is often overlooked is encouraging children to renounce any previous misconceptions in the light of new information. Teachers unfamiliar with the EXEL (Exeter Extending Literacy) project, may find *Writing Frames* by Maureen Lewis and David Wray, (RALIC), or *Developing Children's Non-fiction Writing: Working with Writing Frames* by Maureen Lewis and David Wray (Scholastic), a useful starting point to support their work on non-fiction in the classroom.

Children need a lot of practice before these skills become automatic, so much of this chapter is devoted to this aspect of working with non-fiction. Preliminary work on the characteristic features and evaluation of non-fiction texts is covered in *Curriculum Bank Reading Key Stage 1*, and it is assumed throughout the chapter which follows that children will already have had some experience of these aspects of non-fiction texts. Because of the change in emphasis in the National Curriculum requirements at Key Stage 1, the focus is on science-based activities in this section, namely the body and materials, although the suggestions for skills development can, of course, be applied to any area of the curriculum. For specific suggestions for activities centred on other areas of the curriculum, such as geography, history and art, you can refer to *Curriculum Bank Reading Key Stage 1*.

NAMING PARTS

For the children to: use all available cueing strategies to recognize words in isolation; note similarities and differences between words; match labels to the correct body part; practise Look/Say/Cover/Write/Check routines for learning words; read and use labels with confidence and build sight vocabulary on a specific topic.

†† *Introductory oral session: whole class. Children working in groups. Feedback session: whole class. Practice sessions: pair work.*

🕐 *Introductory oral session: 20 minutes. Group work session: 20–25 minutes. Feedback session: 15–20 minutes. Practice sessions: 10–15 minutes each.*

Previous skills/knowledge needed

It is preferable for children to have experience of listening to each other's views, and contributing their own, in a large group situation. It would also be helpful if they have previous experience of working co-operatively in small groups.

Key background information

To read fluently, accurately and confidently children need to draw on the full range of cueing strategies. To do so, children need plenty of practice in all of these strategies: semantic, syntactic and grapho-phonic.

This activity provides the opportunity for children to build their vocabulary and extend the bank of words that they can recognize on sight. It could usefully form part of a Literacy Hour session, working at word level.

Support children by encouraging them to use all the evidence of the print: to note the length of the word and its shape, the initial letter or blend of letters, to note words within words, to make analogies with words they already know, to note matching patterns and words that rhyme. If the children are not yet familiar with the Look/Say/Cover/Write/Check routine, then you will need to model that with them.

Preparation

It would be interesting for the children to see a skeleton on display. If the school itself does not have one, it is often possible to borrow one from the LEA loan service. Draw the outline of a human body on the flip chart, board or large sheet of paper, ready to add the names of the body parts in the correct places. Write the names of the body parts that you will be introducing on to large labels.

Resources needed

A flip chart, board or large sheet of paper prepared with the outline of a human body, a copy of photocopiable sheets 120 and 121 for each child, writing and drawing materials, the Big Book version of *My Body* by Rhonda Jenkins (Heinemann: *Discovery World*) (optional).

What to do

Tell the children that they will be investigating the human body over the next few sessions. Ask one of the children to come to the front to act as a model and find out which parts of the body the children can already name, starting with the major ones and gradually moving on to the less obvious, for example, head, body, arms, legs, hands, feet, toes, fingers, thumbs, face, eyes, nose, mouth, hair, knees,

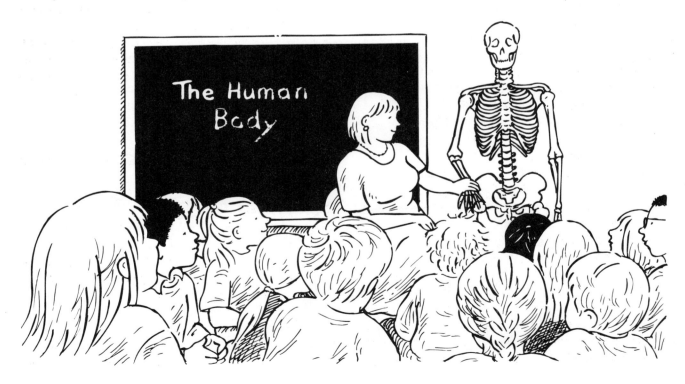

Suggestion(s) for extension

Competent children can play a word-association game, using the names of body parts. Offer a starting word, such as 'head', and the next person has to offer another body part that is associated with it in some way and explain the connection: 'heart' (it begins with the same letter); 'hair' (it grows on the head); 'body' (it is attached to the head); 'brain' (it is inside the head).

Some children could provide dictionary definitions for the body parts and arrange them in alphabetical order to create a glossary. Others could make an activity for their peers to complete, by providing a set of cards with some letters omitted from each body-part word.

Independent readers might like to investigate further by consulting the Moondrake *Body Wise* series by Sharon Cromwell: *Why can't I breathe under water?*, *Why do my feet fall asleep?*, *Why do I shiver when I'm cold?*, *Why do I sweat when I'm hot?*, *What makes bruises 'black and blue'?*.

Suggestion(s) for support

Some children will need the support of an adult to help them complete the sheet.

Others may need a simplified sheet, so you could highlight only those words you expect them to focus on.

An adult could misplace the labels on the body for the children to sort out and return to their correct place, or the children could group together the body parts beginning with the same initial letter.

They could play Pelmanism or Snap with word and picture cards of body parts.

Assessment opportunities

Target any children that you are concerned about and, in the whole-class introductory session, make a mental note of the features that they seem aware of, for example 'My name starts with that letter!' Note any children not attempting to read aloud the labels with the rest of the class, as well as those who can stick the labels in the correct place.

Opportunities for IT

You could use the new words to create a text for 'Developing Tray'.

Display ideas

You could display the outline of the body with accompanying labels and captions, a large version of 'Dem Bones, Dem Bones' song, or mount a display of the collection of poems, rhymes and stories featuring body parts that appear on the class list by the end of the week.

A group of children could go to the school library to gather a set of books about the human body for a classroom display that everyone can browse through at their leisure or use for specific activities later. For instance

shoulders, elbows, neck, chest, back, bottom, waist, ankles, wrists. At this point, you might like to read together the Big Book version of *My Body*. To reinforce the learning, offer, one at a time, the prepared labels and ask individual children to read aloud and stick a label onto the body outline already drawn. Draw attention to any features that might help the children to recognize the words, for example, length, shape, initial letter, spelling pattern. Once all the labels are in place, you could simply read the labels together as a class, or you could go on to play a guessing game, such as: *I am thinking of something beginning with 'm' that we use for eating*, and ask a child to point to and read the appropriate label on the outline of the body.

Divide the children into small groups and hand out photocopiable sheets 120 and 121, asking the children to discuss together and then label the appropriate body parts, referring to the drawing only as a last resort!

Gather the class together at the end of the activity to share the work, and to sing together the 'funny bone' song ('Dem Bones, Dem Bones'). To close the session, provide a large sheet of paper for the children to list, over the week, all the poems, rhymes, story titles they know with the name of a body part in them. Launch the task by scribing one or two on the flip chart to get them going, such as 'Freckly feet and itchy knees' by Michael Rosen.

Organize short slots for partner work during the week for the children to practise with a friend the LSCWC routine to learn to spell and to recognize on sight the new words introduced in the session.

To put new words to good use, as a follow-up activity the children can work on their own to extend the labels into captions, based on their own experiences, for example, 'I hurt my foot at playtime today.' 'I had my hair cut last Saturday.' These could be added to the display.

Dorling Kindersley's *Insight Guide to The Human Body* by Dr Francis Williams; Macdonald Young Books *The Big Book of Bones* by Claire Llewellyn; HarperCollins *Factfinder, Body Facts*; Heinemann *How it Works* series, *Funny Bones* by Anita Ganeri; Oxford Reading Tree *Factfinder, Your Amazing Body* by Roderick Hunt. The pop-up book, *The Human Body*, by Jonathan Miller and David Pelham (Bodley Head) has a special appeal for children!

Other aspects of the English PoS covered

Speaking and listening – 1a, b, c; 2b; 3b.
Writing – 2a, d; 3b.

Reference to photocopiable sheets

The photocopiable sheets 120 and 121 are provided for the children to label correctly the parts of the body and the head. These can be modified by underlining a restricted number of words for those children who are less experienced readers.

WHAT WE CAN DO WITH OUR BODIES

For the children to: read labels and captions competently on a specific topic; read information presented in the form of a Venn diagram; understand the function of verbs; be aware of the number of syllables in words; use strategies for finding information quickly.

†† *Oral session: whole class. Children working in pairs within groups. Feedback session: whole class.*

🕐 *Oral session: 10 minutes. Group/pair work session: 25–30 minutes. Feedback session: 15–20 minutes.*

Previous skills/knowledge needed

It would be helpful if children had experience of evaluating their own and others' work in a supportive manner, and that they were familiar with ways of offering constructive criticism to their peers and of responding to constructive criticism themselves. Preferably, children should already have experience of 'reading' and compiling Venn diagrams.

Key background information

It is important for children to learn how to read information presented in forms other than plain text. It is also important for them to consider the implications of their actions and be able to look at things from someone else's point of view as well as their own, which will stand them in good stead as readers able to interpret sub-text by reading between and beyond the lines.

This activity provides work at text and word level.

Preparation

Provide a collection of books connected with sports and games, healthy exercise, and with early childhood.

Produce enough copies of photocopiable sheet 122 for the children to work in pairs. Fill in the name of a body part for each pair, so that all the major ones are covered by the class overall.

Resources needed

Books collected during 'Preparation', prepared copies of photocopiable sheet 122, a flip chart or board, drawing and writing materials, cards for cue cards.

What to do

To reinforce word recognition skills and awaken children's interest, play a quick oral guessing game: *Tell me three body parts that begin with the same letter / a body part the begins with a silent letter / a body part that rhymes with bed.* Then explain to the children that today the focus is on verbs: you want them to think about all the things we can do with our bodies – with our feet, our hands, our mouths, for instance. You could also ask them to consider

how this has changed since they were born – what can they do now that they could not do when they were tiny babies? Brainstorm a few ideas to whet the children's appetites and write them down on the board or flip chart.

You might like to choose a small selection from the following as a starting point and, if the class is slow to respond, offer a hint or two: write, read, sew, cook, throw and catch, clap, climb, play football, tennis, swim, row a boat, crawl, skip, jump, run, ski, skate, drive a car, ride a bike, read, draw, paint, cuddle, kiss, hug, punch, hit, kick, nip, bite, chew, smell, tickle, smile, comfort, support, frown, threaten.

Briefly discuss the different types of activity – work, play; helpful, hurtful; child, adult; outside, inside – then divide the class into groups of even numbers to explore the ideas further. Children work in pairs within the group. Aim for as wide a range as possible by giving each pair a different body part to focus on. Use the selection of books provided in the classroom and remind them of strategies for finding information as quickly as possible, such as using contents page, index, glossary, and scanning pages with a cue card. Give out a prepared copy of photocopiable sheet 122 to each pair of children and explain how to complete it. They fill in as many appropriate activities as possible, by drawing and/or writing.

After about 25 minutes, bring the class together to share what they have done. The less confident writers could be encouraged to perform ring games, action songs and finger plays to act out what they can do with the body part they

were given on their sheet to reinforce their understanding of verbs. Ask the children if they notice any duplication between the body parts, for instance 'breathing' might appear in the mouth and nose circles, 'running' might appear in the feet and legs circles. Remind or explain to the class how you can show this in a Venn diagram (by overlapping the circles). Do several examples together on the flip chart. Play a quick oral game to provide practice for children in reading a Venn diagram by posing questions, such as: *Which part of the body is used for...? Find something beginning with 'r' that we do with our feet and legs.*

You could also engage in a brief session to develop syllable recognition by asking the children to join in with you as you clap the number of syllables in some of the words. As the children become more confident, you could turn this activity into a guessing game, with the children taking turns to clap the syllables and asking their peers to guess the word they have in mind.

Finally, explore the categories of actions that might be called 'hurtful' and the reasons why people might engage in them – they may be tired, unhappy, lonely, confused. Discuss alternative ways of coping with the anger, annoyance, irritation or misery that everybody feels on a bad day.

Suggestion(s) for extension and support
Children at all levels of competence and experience can take part successfully in this activity.

Assessment opportunities

Note children's ability to classify activities correctly and to associate them with the correct body part. Note their increasing word recognition skills and encourage them to tell you how they recognize words easily. Note also their attempts to spell the known words for body parts in their writing. You can also monitor their awareness of syllables and their ability to interpret information from a Venn diagram.

Opportunities for IT

Children could design their own 'Body Parts' poster, writing a label for each body part and appropriate activities (using verbs), and a list of 'Rules for behaving thoughtfully' for the displays.

Display ideas

The children's suggestions could be displayed on a 'work in progress' board alongside the large Venn diagrams compiled in the whole-class session. Rules for behaving thoughtfully and helpfully could be posted in a prominent place. Children could also create over the week a frieze representing sports, games and work activities, with captions about the parts of the body used in each instance.

Other aspects of the English PoS covered

Speaking and listening – 1a, c, d; 2a, b; 3a.
Writing – 1a, b; 2a, c, d, e; 3a.

Reference to photocopiable sheet

Photocopiable sheet 122 requires children to focus on verbs. They make a collection of the actions associated with a specific part of the body.

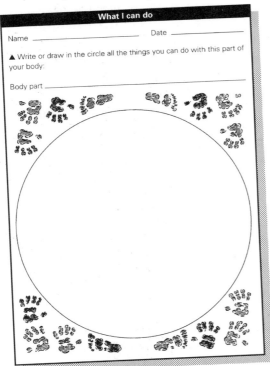

What I can do

Name _____ Date _____

▲ Write or draw in the circle all the things you can do with this part of your body:

Body part: _____

KEEPING FIT

For the children to: formulate and read aloud questions on a specific topic; explore different ways of representing information; interpret meaning from graphs and charts.

†† *Introductory oral session: whole class. Preparation and survey sessions: whole class, then children working in pairs. Pooling of results session: whole class. Drawing graphs and charts session: children working in groups.*

🕐 *Introductory oral session: 30–40 minutes. Preparation and survey sessions: 15–20 minutes each. Pooling of results session: 20–25 minutes. Drawing graphs and charts session: 30 minutes.*

Previous skills/knowledge needed

Children should be accustomed to moving about the school in a responsible manner and be able to work with some independence in order to carry out the survey. Preferably, they should have previous experience of formulating appropriate questions for a questionnaire and working with graphs.

Key background information

Children need to know that information comes in a variety of forms, such as diagrams, charts, graphs, maps, logos and pictures, as well as words. Teachers have to help them to become confident and competent in interpreting information when they confront it in all of these forms.

This activity provides work at sentence and text level.

Preparation

You will need to negotiate with other members of staff before sending off your class to carry out the survey round the school. If your class is inexperienced at composing questionnaires, you will need some examples of questionnaires from previous classes to show to the children. Collect some examples from books and pamphlets of different ways of drawing up graphs and charts.

For extension activities, you need also to have a selection of pamphlets about the leisure facilities available in your area.

Resources needed

A flip chart or board, a clipboard per pair of children, examples of questionnaires, graphs and charts, writing materials, a copy of *Exercise and Your Health* by Jillian Powell (Wayland *Health Matters* series) (optional).

What to do

Gather together as a whole class to launch the session. Talk to the children about the body as a kind of machine, like a car, that has to last a very long time, and, just like a car, has to be looked after by changing the oil, checking the engine, cleaning the plugs, and so on, our bodies have to be looked after too so that they can keep on working efficiently.

Ask the children to share any ideas they have about how to keep their bodies fit. They might suggest eating sensibly, getting plenty of sleep, not taking risks that could lead to an accident, wearing appropriate clothing, having a warm dry home to live in, taking regular exercise. Tell the class that you are now going to focus on exercise in this session and, acting as scribe, brainstorm and list on the flip chart the exercise the children already take that helps to keep them fit and healthy: walking, skipping, playing games, swimming, going to gym club, and so on. Remind them that these are all **verbs**, describing what we **do**.

Ask if anyone in their family, or perhaps a family friend, takes regular exercise to keep in shape – works in the garden, works out at a gym, goes to aerobics classes, line-dances, plays for a local football or netball team, plays golf or cricket, jogs, takes the dog for a walk, and so on. Again, scribe their contributions on the flip chart. You could show and discuss *Exercise and Your Health* to see if any new ideas crop up that the children had not thought of.

Explain that the class is going to carry out a survey of all the people in the school to find out how, when and why they and their families exercise… or not, as the case may be! Several sessions will be needed during the week to draft the questionnaire, discuss and agree upon the format, word process and photocopy the questionnaire, and organize and carry out the survey.

First of all you will need to draft a questionnaire together. Show the children the examples you have ready and/or remind them of previous questionnaires they have composed. Highlight the key question words, such as Who? Where? When? How (often/easy/difficult/far/long)? What? Why? Remind them to use question marks.

You will also need to discuss ways of making the questionnaire as easy as possible to complete, for example, a tick-list format – perhaps with columns for all possible activities for the children themselves and for someone in their family. You might also like to draw their attention to the need for being able to extract useful information later on, such as variations in responses due to gender, age or disability; the effect that the availability of facilities in the area has on responses, as well as ease of access to the facilities and the cost; people's attitudes – how important they think keeping fit is.

Once the format has been finalized, word-process it or ask a competent group of children to do so, then make one photocopy of the result for each pair. Then, organize the children into pairs and make out a schedule for them to go around the school with the finished questionnaire to carry out the survey. Make sure they do not forget to question all the staff as well as the children.

At the end of the week, meet as a whole class to share the results of the survey and collate the findings. Show the children a few examples of different ways of drawing up charts and graphs in books and talk about the ease of scanning them for information. Some groups might like to represent their findings in different ways, such as tally chart, bar graph, pictorial graph.

Divide the children into groups to be responsible for representing the responses in an easily accessible format: children's favourite form of exercise; the exercise adults, boys, girls, senior citizens, disabled people prefer; factors affecting people's participation in regular exercise; views on the importance of keeping fit. Display the completed work where everyone in the school can see it.

Finally, recap on just how successful the survey was: Were the questions clear? Were there any omissions? Was the information easy to collect and to note? Which format was easiest for representing the results? Which was easiest to interpret?

Suggestion(s) for extension

Drawing on the selection of pamphlets you have collected, independent readers and writers could plan a brochure to promote regular exercise, spelling out the reasons and consequences, and offering advice on how you can keep fit, on your own, with friends, at home or out and about.

Suggestion(s) for support

Before carrying out the survey, some children will need to practise with an adult or more experienced peer, in order to be able to read the questions fluently

Some children will benefit from teacher guidance when drawing up their graphs/charts.

Assessment opportunities

Note children's ability to formulate relevant questions and to read them aloud, their confidence in carrying out the survey and reporting back to the class. Note also their growing awareness of the appropriate format for representing information and their ability to interpret it.

Opportunities for IT

Children could be responsible for word-processing the survey questionnaire. Some groups might like to use IT to produce their charts and graphs. Brochures (see 'Suggestion(s) for extension') could be produced using a DTP program.

Display ideas

The results of the survey should be displayed in a prominent position in the school entrance, perhaps where parents and visitors can read them.

A large display of paintings, models, pieces of writing, examples of special clothing and equipment could be mounted in the school hall to promote regular healthy exercise.

Other aspects of the English PoS covered

Speaking and listening – 1a, c; 2a, b.
Writing – 1a, c; 2a, b, c, d, e.

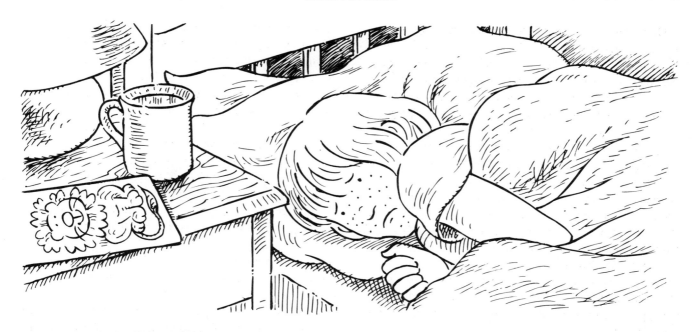

ILLNESSES AND ACCIDENTS

For the children to: scan a chart quickly in order to answer questions; use pictures as an aid to scanning for information; observe a picture carefully and infer meaning from the sub-text, going beyond the literal; read their own writing aloud to the class.

†† Session One: *Oral session: whole class. Writing session: children working on their own. Feedback session: whole class.* **Session Two**: *Oral session: whole class. Children working individually or in small groups.*

⊕ Session One: *Oral session: 15–20 minutes. Writing session: 20–25 minutes. Feedback session: 5–10 minutes.* **Session Two**: *Oral session: 20-25 minutes. Individual/group work session: 30 minutes.*

Previous skills/knowledge needed
It would be helpful if children already had some experience of looking intently at pictures and were aware of the need to read beyond the literal.

Key background information
'Reading' pictures is an essential skill that is often neglected, yet children need just as much practice in interpreting images as they do words. Lists are also a crucial part of literacy development as they help us to organize our thoughts and shape our ideas so that we can communicate our meaning effectively to our readers.

This activity covers work at text level.

Preparation
Arrange a display of an assortment of fiction and non-fiction books connected with childhood illnesses and accidents for the children to browse through.

Send off for samples of pamphlets about childhood illnesses and accident prevention from the local Health Authority.

Resources needed
Books and literature on childhood illnesses and accidents, a flip chart or board, paper and writing materials, a copy of photocopiable sheet 123 for each child.

What to do
Session One
Explain to the children that sometimes, no matter how carefully we look after our bodies, something goes wrong – we might pick up a virus – and we fall ill. Ask the children in turn to tell you of any illnesses they themselves have had, read about or heard about – rashes, measles, chicken pox, scarlet fever, mumps, whooping cough, cold, flu, eye or ear infections, rheumatic fever, diarrhoea, diphtheria. Perhaps they remember having injections at a clinic to prevent them getting certain illnesses.

Together, compile a chart of illnesses on the flip chart and mark those suffered by children in your class, which you can use later for quick oral quizzes in the odd spare moment. For instance: *Look carefully at the chart and tell me how many children in the class have had chicken pox? Which illness has no one in our class had? Has anyone had diphtheria?*

Ask the children to say how they felt when they were ill – sore, in severe pain, worried, bored, tired, sick, itchy, frightened, frustrated, and so on. Ask them to think about the things that helped them to feel better or cheer them up – medicines, ointments, get-well cards, presents, visits, treats, being read to, having someone to play with, watching television, listening to tapes, watching the world out of the window, writing to friends and family, having telephone calls from friends.

Talk about visits to the doctor or an out-patients department or longer stays in hospital. What are the most significant memories that children have of these occasions? Can they think of a pleasant or funny incident as well as an unhappy one?

When you have aired a range of ideas and stirred children's memories or imaginations, set the children to write about a time when they were ill, real or imagined.

Gather together at the end of the session for children to read their writing to the class. Encourage the children to offer supportive comments on each other's work, saying which part they liked best, which phrases appealed to them, how well the story unfolded, what an interesting start it had, how well the story ended, how humorous it was, how the dialogue sounded just right, and so on.

Session Two
Compliment the children on their work on illness, and explain that today you are going to move on to consider other setbacks to health, that is, accidents. Ask the class to tell you about any accidents that occurred in their home, or at school or on holiday. List on the flip chart all the accidents and how they happened, for example breaking a leg by tripping over the dog in the park. When all accidents have been recorded, check through the list to note the different kinds of accidents – heat causing burns and scalds; falls causing fractures, sprains, bruises and cuts; trapped limbs causing breaks, torn ligaments, bruises and cuts, dislocations; swallowing things causing breathing difficulties, blockages, vomiting; bites causing cuts, bruises, inflammation, even blood poisoning.

Tell the children that the best way to prevent accidents from happening is to look carefully at what caused the

accident and then try to remove the trigger so that it won't happen again, for example the school rule that no one must run is precisely to prevent children from bumping into one another at high speed, causing broken limbs or head injuries. Share with the class a few pictures of home life in books or on posters and ask them to point out any possible hazards.

Ask them to think carefully about each area of their own house, especially the kitchen, to spot potential hazards, bearing in mind the different types of accidents talked about earlier – a trailing flex, badly balanced pans, badly placed kettles, things on high shelves, poisonous substances in low cupboards, loose carpets and mats, sharp knives, fireguards, window locks, stair gates, and so on. Then, hand out photocopiable sheet 123 depicting a kitchen scene with deliberate hazards shown. The children complete it by circling all the hazards they spot, and then list ways of preventing accidents. This task can be done in small groups.

Suggestion(s) for extension
Fluent readers could use the pamphlets on accident prevention or childhood illnesses for a group reading and discussion session. They could then be asked to report on their new knowledge to the class.

Suggestion(s) for support
When working on photocopiable sheet 123, some children will need an adult to guide them with prompt questions, such as: *Can you see anything sticking out that someone might fall over? Who can see something that might catch fire? Can you see anything dangerous that hasn't been put away properly?*

Assessment opportunities

Note children's ability to interpret the chart of the class's illnesses in order to answer your oral questions in Session One, and their ability to infer meaning from pictures when working with the photocopiable sheet.

Opportunities for IT

Children could compile a glossary of childhood illnesses or design an accident prevention poster.

Display ideas

An initial display of pamphlets from the local Health Authority on childhood diseases, together with large photographs or posters showing children in hospital or ill in bed at home, would help to engage the children's interest in the topic, as well as encouraging them to read different types of text. Children's personal accounts of their illnesses could be displayed with accompanying drawings, paintings or family photographs.

Other aspects of the English PoS covered

Speaking and listening – 1a, c; 2a, b.
Writing – 1a, b, c; 2a, b, c, d, e.

Reference to photocopiable sheet

Children are required to look carefully at the picture on photocopiable sheet 123 depicting a kitchen scene in order to identify and circle possible hazards and suggest accident prevention measures.

A HEALTHY DIET

For the children to: revisit dictionary skills; identify simple questions and use structural guiders in a non-fiction text to locate information effectively; use a key-word scanning card to find relevant information quickly; to identify the main points and gist of a text by noting or underlining; evaluate information from a range of sources; to recognize that non-fiction books on similar themes can give different information; practise scanning charts to retrieve information quickly.

†† *Session One: Introductory session: whole class. Library session: pair work. Session Two: Research session: pair work. Feedback session: whole class. Session Three: Oral session: whole class. Writing session: children working individually. Feedback session: whole class.*

🕐 *Session One: Introductory session: 20 minutes. Library session: 15–20 minutes. Session Two: Research session: 10 minutes. Feedback session: 30 minutes. Session Three: Oral session: 10 minutes. Writing session: 20 minutes. Feedback session: 5–10 minutes.*

Previous skills/knowledge needed

Children should already have experience of working with non-fiction texts and be aware of how to use the structural features in a non-fiction book, such as an index, contents page, headings, captions, and so on.

Key background information

Exeter University's EXEL research programme has proved invaluable in helping us to support children's 'reading to learn' skills development. A systematic six step approach can be very effective:
▲ Find out what they know already.
▲ Decide what they want to find out – generating a set of questions is most effective for this stage (What? Who? Where? When? Why? How?).
▲ Locate and select relevant information – library skills, text marking, scanning with key-word cue cards.
▲ Evaluate information – compare and contrast information from a range of sources.
▲ Adapt thinking in the light of new knowledge – what have they learned?
▲ Organize information to suit purposes – choose the appropriate format for presenting information, such as account, diary, chart, diagram, model, poster.

This activity entails work at text, sentence and word levels.

Preparation

Keep a dictionary to hand for Session One.

Make small key-word cue cards (bookmark size seems ideal for Key Stage 1) for each child to use to scan the

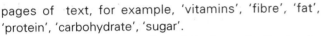

pages of text, for example, 'vitamins', 'fibre', 'fat', 'protein', 'carbohydrate', 'sugar'.

Some suggestions to look out for when selecting books for Session Two are:
▲ Wayland *Health Matters* series
Food and Your Health by Jillian Powell
▲ Wayland *Food Facts* series
Vitamins, *Fats* and *Sugar*, all by Rhoda Nottridge
Fibre and *Protein*, both by Jane Inglis
▲ Wayland *Food* series by Jillian Powell
Rice, *Poultry*, *Fruit*, *Vegetables*, *Milk*, *Fish*, *Potatoes*;
▲ Heinemann Library *Food in Focus* series
Beans and Pulses by Roz Denny
Fruit and Vegetables and *Bread* by Jenny Ridgewell
Milk and *Yoghurt* by Hazel King
▲ Heinemann *Images* series
Food by Karen Bryant-Mole
▲ A&C Black *Linkers* series
Food discovered through Science by Karen Bryant-Mole.

Most reading packages also include non-fiction books these days, for instance Oxford Reading Tree: *Keeping Healthy* and *What Should You Eat?* by John Foster, *Amazing Food Facts* by Fiona Macdonald, *Ice cream* by Valerie Fawcett. Longmans Book Project *Science in the Kitchen* has Big Book versions of *Ice Cream* by Dave Byrne and Mike Wheeler and the starter book *Food* by Bobbie Neate.

Resources needed

A flip chart or board, a dictionary, card to make cue-cards, writing materials, books on healthy eating, a copy of photocopiable sheet 124 for each child, access to the library.

What to do

Session One

Explain to the children that they will be looking in detail at the role a healthy diet plays in keeping their bodies in good working order. First, find out the children's perceptions about what constitutes a healthy diet and scribe their thoughts in two columns onto the flip chart: 'Healthy' and 'Unhealthy'. Which foods do the children believe to be healthy and which do they consider to be unhealthy? Make sure all the children have a chance to air their views about the foods they like – fish fingers, sausages, milk shakes, chips, bread, buns, apple tart, vegetable curry, chocolate, biscuits, cakes, ice cream, lemonade – and make a note of everything to refer back to later.

Next, introduce the terms 'protein', 'carbohydrate', 'fat', 'vitamins', if the children have not already mentioned them. Read out definitions of these words from a dictionary, modelling as you do so how to find your way around a dictionary easily. For instance you could ask the children where in the alphabet a specific initial letter comes – near the beginning, middle or end. You could draw their attention to the guide words at the top of a page and comment on strict alphabetical order, once you have found the initial letter. Take suggestions as to which of the foods on the chart contain any of these four elements – does ice cream have protein in it… fat, carbohydrate, vitamins? See if there is a pattern emerging – is any element featuring more regularly in the healthy list, or vice versa?

It is now time to consider how accurate our views are! *Where did we get our information from – friends, television, family, advertisements? How can we be sure that our opinions are correct? Everyone makes mistakes sometimes! Shouldn't we be wary of believing something without checking it out for ourselves?* As a class, go to the school library and, in pairs, locate books on the subject of healthy eating, highlighting the appropriate Dewey number or school colour code. Select a large variety of books to take back to the classroom (see 'Preparation') for further, more careful, reading in the next session to compare information from a range of sources.

Session Two

In this session, use the books selected previously (see 'Preparation') and remind the class how to use the structural features in a non-fiction book such as the index, contents, captions, headings and so on, to find relevant sections of a text quickly. Introduce a key-word cue card, showing how you draw this down the centre of the page line by line, your eyes quickly scanning from right to left to see if the target word appears. If it does, stop and read that section of text more carefully, but if not, proceed until you find the specific information you are looking for.

Divide the class into pairs, giving each pair a specific target to find out about – protein, fat, energy, vitamins, fibre. On the flip chart, quickly brainstorm some key questions to support the children's research, such as: *What is protein? Where is it found? Who needs it? How much is needed? Why is it needed?* Then hand out the cue-cards with the key-word printed on them. Allow them ten minutes to scan the books and underline or jot down in note form the most important points.

Ask the children to read out their notes and discuss with them any differences between the various sources of information and check whether their original thoughts were borne out by their book-searches. Stress what they have learned, what they now know to be accurate that they were unsure, or even wrong, about before. It is important to make agreed alterations on the original flip chart to correct any misconceptions the children might have had. Aim to ensure that by the end of the session children understand that the body needs all of these elements – fat, carbohydrate, protein, vitamins – to function properly but that moderation is the key to success. Recap on the steps they took to find information: locate the appropriate part of book by using structural guiders; find specific information by using a scanning cue card; note or underline main points and useful details; reject misconceptions and assimilate new knowledge!

Finally, ask the children to keep a diary of everything they eat in the following week, so that next week you will be able to check that you are all – teacher included – eating a healthy diet that will keep your body machine in good working order.

Session Three

Gather the whole class together to check the food value of what you have eaten in the previous week. Using your own diary as an exemplar, write in the columns headed 'Healthy' and 'Unhealthy' on the flip chart, as in Session One, all the items you have eaten day by day through the week, then complete each column with what the children have eaten. Refer to the class collection of books as necessary to check on any items you are unsure about.

Hand out the photocopiable sheets 124 for the children to complete their own personal grid of the food value of what they have eaten during the week. They can consult a friend or books to check any item they are unsure of.

When everyone has finished, ask the children to swap their chart with a friend so they can read each other's. As a class, discuss how easy it was to interpret the charts. Did anyone have any difficulties? What could be improved next time? Were more columns needed? Were the spaces big enough? Would it be easier with the axes reversed?

Suggestion(s) for extension

Confident readers could be encouraged to go to their local library to find more books on the subject of healthy eating. They could prepare a handbook spelling out the vitamins, fat, protein, carbohydrate contained in their favourite recipes or prepare a pamphlet for vegetarians to ensure they understand the levels of protein and so on in the foods they eat.

For further practice in research skills, some children might like to investigate a different aspect on their own, for example how the body processes the food we eat – *Under the Microscope: Digesting how we fuel our body* by Angela Royston (Franklin Watts) would be of help here. Perhaps they could look at environmental issues, in which case Wayland *Environment Starts Here!, Food* by Brenda Williams would come in useful; food for special occasions, in which case the Oxford Reading Tree *Factfinder, Festival Food* would be a good starting point; food in different parts of the world…

Suggestion(s) for support

In Session Two, some children will need the reassurance of working on texts with a partner. They would also benefit from using an acetate sheet to underline parts of the text instead of having to make notes.

Some children might need the support of an adult to help them complete their food diary grid.

Assessment opportunities

You can monitor children's skills in locating information using the structural guides in non-fiction texts and their scanning skills when using the cue cards. Note children's spelling strategies when engaged in writing activities, and their ability to read aloud from their grids when reporting back to the class.

Opportunities for IT

A DTP program could be used for a professional finish for food charts.

Display ideas

Food charts could form the basis of a general display on healthy eating, incorporating recipes, shopping lists, relevant poems and stories and still-life paintings. These could be linked with the regular exercise display from the 'Keeping fit' activity on page 72 if appropriate.

A poster could be displayed reminding children of the steps to take when researching a topic.

Other aspects of English PoS covered

Speaking and listening – 1a, b, c; 2a, b; 3b.
Writing – 1a, b, c; 2a, b, c, d, e; 3a.

Reference to photocopiable sheet

Photocopiable sheet 124 is in the form of a chart for the children to keep a record of the kinds of food they eat in one week. They will use it to try to interpret information 'at a glance'.

What I have eaten

Name _____   Date _____

▲ Write down everything you eat this week and put a tick in the appropriate column to show its value.

Food	Protein	Vitamins	Carbohydrate	Fibre	Fat
Monday					
Tuesday					
Thursday					
Friday					
Saturday					
Sunday					

KEEPING OUR BODIES COMFORTABLE

For the children to: develop confidence and competence in using the Dewey system or school colour-coded system to locate books; develop information retrieval skills, using structural features of non-fiction texts; to skim-read a book in order to find out what it is about; read reflectively to take on board new knowledge and remember it.

†† *Introductory oral session: whole class. Library session: whole class. Children working in pairs. Writing session: group and individual work.*

🕐 *Introductory oral session: 10–15 minutes. Library session: 25 minutes. Pair work session: 10 minutes. Writing session: 30–40 minutes.*

Previous skills/knowledge needed
An earlier introduction to using a library would be helpful, as would some experience in researching a topic.

Key background information
For children to feel confident and competent in using a library effectively, they need considerable experience of using the Dewey or equivalent cataloguing system.

Children also need to be able to read in different ways for different purposes. When faced with non-fiction texts they have to read reflectively to take on board new knowledge and remember it. They need plenty of opportunities in meaningful situations to learn those skills that are essential for study, skills that have to become automatic if children are to be successful learners across the curriculum. This activity covers work at text, sentence and word levels.

Preparation
Collect clothes, hats and footwear for wearing in cold and hot weather to help keep the body temperature stable, ready for the class to use to mount a display.

Resources needed
Card and felt-tipped pens for making labels and captions, examples of clothing and footwear, access to the library.

What to do
Tell the children that you are going to talk about body temperature. Explain how important this is – if the human body gets too hot or too cold it cannot work properly. First of all, find out what the children already know, then discuss the questions that might guide their research: *Which materials are waterproof? Who needs special protection? How do some materials keep the body cooler than others? Why are layers more effective for keeping the body warm?* Mention also key cue words, such as 'protection', 'sunscreen', 'waterproof', 'windproof'.

Go to the school library and ask the children to work in pairs to locate as many books as possible about appropriate protective clothing for cold and hot weather. Ask them in which section of the library the books are likely to be found, then discuss strategies for finding out quickly whether books will be relevant to their purpose or not – look at the title, cover blurb, contents, index; quickly skim through a text from cover to cover to see if there is sufficient relevant information in it to warrant a more careful read; compare one book with another to see which will be more use.

Remind the children to be as wide-ranging as possible; to include clothing in other parts of the world where the climate is very different from our own and where different cultural traditions might hold sway. Remind them also that expectations about clothing might vary according to gender and age too. Allow them about 10 minutes to select books, then talk together for a further 15 minutes to check if their initial ideas were correct and to find out what else they have learned so far.

Transfer the books to the classroom so that everyone has a chance to consult all relevant books during the week.

Show the children the clothes you have collected and ask them to work in pairs to sort them out ready to mount two displays – one for clothes to keep us warm and/or dry in cold weather, and one for clothes to keep us cool and protect us from the sun in hot weather. Ask the children to bring in any relevant pieces of clothing from home to add to the display.

Children will be expected to make labels for the clothing, and, when their research is completed, to write captions to explain why the particular piece of clothing is effective. They could use any extra information they discover to make a 'Did you know?' corner for the display, and lists of 'dos' and 'dont's' for winter and summer.

As a follow-up activity you might like to set up a hat, shoe or clothes shop in the classroom for children to engage in role-play activities, and to provide them with opportunities for writing price labels, bills, sale notices, cheques, refund tickets, and so on.

Over the week, you could also read some fictional stories involving clothes such as the Edward Lear poem 'The Quangle Wangle's Hat', Tomi Ungerer's 'The Hat', 'The Elves and the Shoemaker', the section about the mad hatter's tea party from *Alice in Wonderland*. You could condense and tell the very funny story-with-a moral about the stolen balaclava from George Layton's *The Fib* short-story collection (Penguin).

Suggestion(s) for extension
Confident readers could find and read dictionary definitions for specialized pieces of clothing, for example skiing goggles, moon boots and/or make up their own definitions to include in the display.

Some children might like to find information books that will help them to investigate the dangers that exist for old people in cold weather conditions because of hypothermia. Others could make a quiz game with question cards based on the properties of clothes.

Suggestion(s) for support
You may need to work with the more inexperienced readers in the library session. Some children will require adult support in composing captions for the display.

Assessment opportunities
Note children's confidence in using the library and their ability to select appropriate books, as well as their information retrieval skills when scanning the books for information on clothing. Monitor their reading and writing strategies when making their caption cards.

Opportunities for IT
All items for the display, such as labels, captions, definitions, headings and sub-headings could be produced on the computer to good effect.

Display ideas
Mount clothes with accompanying labels and captions as suggested above.

Other areas of PoS covered
Speaking and listening – 2a, b.
Writing – 1b, c; 2a, b.

WOOD

For children to: develop awareness of linguistic features that support comprehension; develop skills for reading aloud to large groups; further develop research strategies.

**†† ** *Oral sessions: whole class. Drawing sessions: individual or in groups. Writing sessions: children working on their own. Visit preparatory, research and writing sessions: whole class, group and individual work.*

⏰ *Oral sessions: 5 minutes each. Drawing sessions: 15 minutes each. Writing sessions: 15–20 minutes each. Visit preparatory session: 20–25 minutes; research session: 30 minutes; writing session: 45–60 minutes.*

Previous skills/knowledge needed

Children whose interest in language has already been awakened and who are used to talking about and playing with language will respond more readily to this activity. But we all have to start somewhere!

Key background information

To become discriminating readers and writers, it is important for children to acquire close observational skills, paying careful attention to details, noting thoughtful choices of vocabulary, varied syntax, use of punctuation, cohesive links. 'Publishing' their own writing contributes to children's understanding of linguistic features that promote clarity, accessibility and interest for a reader.

This activity includes work at text, sentence and word levels.

Preparation

Assemble an initial collection of wooden objects (see 'What to do' and a display of books about wood.

If a visit is to be undertaken, then the usual careful preparation must be made for that, such as arranging transport, if necessary; checking times with the museum; organizing accompanying adults; obtaining written permission from parents; going through with the children the behaviour and safety rules when out and about; discussing suitable clothing; preparing clipboards, sketch paper and tools for use during the visit.

Resources needed

Drawing materials (including charcoal and sketch paper), wooden objects and books about wood, a flip chart or board, writing materials, clipboards, cameras and film (optional), access to the library.

What to do

Tell the children you are going to look at wood. Ask if they know where it comes from. During the week, amass a collection of wooden objects by searching at home yourself and asking children and colleagues to bring in items from home too. Aim for a varied selection, to include different types of wood; tools for different purposes; artefacts from different parts of the world; wood worked and finished in different ways, such as cooking spoons, serving bowls and boards, toys, puppets, ornaments, boxes, marquetry pictures, clocks, jewellery, musical instruments, doll's furniture, mirrors, picture frames, and photographs of homes, furniture, sculptures, totem poles, transport on land and sea, windmills, waterwheels, farm implements.

Over the next few days, look closely at a few of the objects at the start of morning and afternoon sessions, describing them in detail and talking about their fitness for purpose, and, in some cases, their replacement by more modern equipment. Consult books from the collection on display to verify points or expand knowledge as necessary. Any new vocabulary or technical terms such as 'lacquer', 'marquetry', 'lathe', and so on can be noted on the flip chart. The children can use dictionaries to find accurate definitions afterwards, and practise the LSCWC routine during the week to consolidate spelling.

Allow set times for the children to draw, in groups or on their own, a chosen artefact and write about it – first, a full description, then who brought it in, how long they have had it in their home, how and when it was made, what it is used for, what alternatives there are for doing the same job, and so on. Encourage children to choose their vocabulary carefully, vary their sentence construction, sequence sentences carefully, and punctuate accurately in order to provide clarity and interest for their readers.

Try to arrange a visit to a relevant nearby place of interest, such as a watermill, a windmill, a transport museum, a museum of rural life, a toy museum, (all of which house many objects made of wood) so that the children can record in photographs, observational drawings and writing what they learn from their visits.

On their return, children can find appropriate books from the school library to add to any pamphlets obtained on their visit and compile a booklet to include the historical, social, scientific aspects of toys, farms, transport, waterwheels, and so on, depending on the visit undertaken. Remind children of the 'what? where? when? who? why? how?' questions that will help them to find the information they are looking for.

As a follow-up activity, children could report to the school in an assembly. They will need time to practise their reading aloud skills before the event. Draw their attention to audibility and clarity, to the speed of delivery, variety of intonation and the effect of emphasis and pauses.

Suggestion(s) for extension

Using the systematic stages for researching a topic as set out in the introduction to this book, competent readers and writers could pursue individual or group interests and investigate, say, furniture, boats, instruments through the ages, houses across the world, finishing up by 'publishing' a non-fiction book of their own to add to the class library.

Suggestion(s) for support

Astute pairing for the visit will enable an experienced partner to support a less experienced child.

Some children will need to be guided through the steps for researching a topic – perhaps by having an adult prompter working alongside, or by referring to a poster on the classroom wall with the steps written out.

Assessment opportunities

Monitor children's increasing familiarity with a systematic approach to researching topics, in some cases with some measure of independence. Note their vocabulary choices and thoughtful language use in their written work.

Note also their growing confidence, accuracy, audibility, flow and meaningful intonation in reading aloud to a large audience.

Opportunities for IT

Children will benefit from using a computer to 'publish' their booklets.

Display ideas

The initial display of artefacts made of wood should be a central attraction in the classroom. Later you can help children to mount a wall display of their drawings and accompanying descriptions.

A table display of the various groups' published books and pamphlets should preferably be arranged where children from other classes can browse through them and enjoy them too.

Other areas of the English PoS covered

Speaking and listening – 1c; 2a, b; 3a.
Writing – 1a, b, c; 2b, c, d, e; 3a, b.

A WALK IN THE WOODS

For the children to: develop independent research skills, by using a simple writing frame; use the structural guiders in a non-fiction book to locate information quickly; write a non-fiction book, providing structural guiders for readers.

†† *Preparation session: whole class. Writing and research sessions: children working in groups. Final session: whole class.*

🕐 *Preparation session: 15 minutes. Time the walk plus journey to and from school. Writing and research sessions: 30 minutes each. Final session: 25–30 minutes.*

Previous skills/knowledge needed

It would be helpful if children already had experience of out-of-school visits and were aware of the potential hazards, especially if the wood is by a stretch of water. Also, it would be beneficial if they were aware of environmental issues, such as climbing trees, picking wild flowers and berries, and so on. Some familiarity with maps would be useful, as well as previous use of writing frames to support learning.

Preparation

Encourage the children to share in the preparation for the outing, and make sure every organizational feature is taken care of. (See the earlier points in 'Wood' about preparing to take children off the school premises.) Autumn is a good time to choose for a walk in the woods, as the colours are at their best and seeds and such are plentiful. Make a collection of relevant books, for example on the identification of trees, seed dispersal, seasonal changes, wildlife of woods and parks, instructions for planting seeds, and so on.

Resources needed

For the outing: paper, writing and drawing materials for bark rubbing, sketching and making notes, clipboards, camera and film.

In class: book collection (see 'Preparation'), materials for planting seeds (small plant pots, soil or compost, watering can, labels), a copy of photocopiable sheet 125 for each child, writing paper and writing materials, a flip chart or board.

Key background information

It is a teacher's responsibility to ensure that children have experience of reading and writing a full range of different text types. This activity provides experience in researching a topic using a simple writing frame, based on first hand experience and secondary sources. It also provides opportunities for the children to write lists, letters, sets of rules, descriptions, non-fiction texts.

What to do

Tell the children that you are going to look at trees at first hand. Discuss the visit to the nearby wood or the local park and decide what you will need to take with you, and what it would be appropriate to wear. Together, compose a letter to parents, giving all the necessary information, requesting formal permission for each child to go, and asking for volunteers to accompany you on the walk. It

will be wise to stress to the children that they must never go for a walk on their own, without an adult they already know well, or without the permission of their family.

Before you set off, remind the children to use their senses well, to 'look with intent', to listen carefully (not to chatter loudly or they won't hear anything and they will scare wildlife away!), to feel textures of tree trunks carefully, to smell deeply – but not to taste! Explain why, if the children do not already know.

Tell them to note anything of interest, such as colours of leaves, spiralling falling leaves, patterns on bark, moss, fungi, to keep an eye open for squirrels, rabbits, birds; to note the noise of leaves under foot, of the wind in the branches; to compare the smell of damp undergrowth, pine trees, wild flowers. Remind them to sketch anything they feel is interesting as well as making notes, and to take care when making their bark rubbings to get a good, clear rubbing, not a slapdash smear, without damaging the bark. In consultation with an adult, they are to collect a variety of fallen seeds to bring back to school for planting.

On your return to school, talk about what you found out on your walk, then divide the children into groups according to the areas of investigation they want to pursue further, such as seed dispersal, wildlife in trees, tree varieties, seasonal cycle, planting seeds. Hand out copies

of photocopiable sheet 125 and brainstorm with the children a few questions that they might want answered. Write these on the flip chart. The children then work in their small groups or pairs within a group, using the books from your collection, to complete their research before going on to write non-fiction texts, which will be added to the display about their outing . Attractive headings; all the preliminary planning notes and letters; the sketches, notes and rubbings from the walk, with labels and explanatory captions attached; the potted seeds with 'how to' instructions about planting, and ongoing comments as they grow; photographs of the outing with the children's written accounts alongside can all be included in the display.

Suggestion(s) for extension

Experienced readers could undertake a co-operative project to investigate environmental factors pertaining to forests world-wide, the dangers and the possible solutions, and then write a text of their own for their peers, remembering to supply a contents page, index and so on, as befits a non-fiction text, and to include a map showing the position of the world's remaining large areas of forests.

They could prepare a group reading of Jeannie Baker's *Where the Forest Meets the Sea* (Walker), which spells out the dangers of the disappearing rain forests in Australia.

Suggestion(s) for support

Give careful thought to the group tasks: some children would benefit from a more straightforward writing task such as listing what is needed for planting seeds, then sequencing the steps of the instructions correctly.

Assessment opportunities

Note children's facility in using the supplied writing frame to support their research work, their growing ability to ask appropriate questions; also their ability to use structural guiders in the books they consult, and to provide those same guiders when they write non-fiction texts of their own.

Opportunities for IT

There are many opportunities here for children to compose using IT – lists, letters, labels, captions, accounts, instructions, and non-fiction books.

Display ideas

Mount a full report of the outing and subsequent work as described in 'What to do'.

Other aspects of English PoS covered

Speaking and listening – 1a, c; 2b; 3b.
Writing – 1a, c; 2b, c, d, e; 3a, b.

Reference to photocopiable sheet

Photocopiable sheet 125 provides a basic framework to support children as they research a topic.

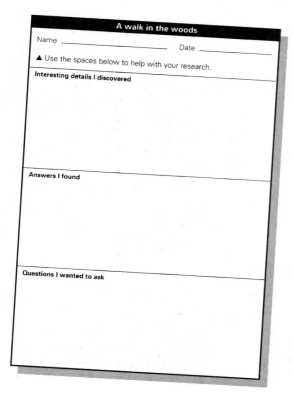

FROM TREES TO TABLES

For the children to: use a range of cueing strategies to read an unknown text; reorder a text in a logical sequence; scan books for relevant information on a given topic; be aware of the characteristics of process writing.

†† *Browsing session: children working in small groups. Oral session: whole class. Writing session: individual or pair work.*

🕐 *Browsing session: 10 minutes. Oral session: 25–30 minutes. Writing session: 20–25 minutes.*

Previous skills/knowledge needed

It would be helpful if children had already come across other processes, such as the story of bread-making. (See the 'Little Red Hen' activity in *Curriculum Bank English Key Stage 1*.)

Key background information

Children need experience of reading a whole range of different genres before they can be expected to make appropriate choices about formats for their own writing.

This activity provides an opportunity for work at text level. It requires children to explain a process, and will help them to understand the importance of correct sequencing of events.

Preparation

Select books about wood to share amongst the children, such as Terry Jennings *Wood* (A&C Black), Catherine Chambers *Wood and Bark* (in the *Would You Believe It!* series from Evans Brothers), Henry Pluckrose *Wood* (Watts).

Resources needed

A selection of books about wood (see 'Preparation'), a flip chart, paper and writing materials, a copy of photocopiable sheet 126 for less experienced children.

What to do

Explain to the children that you will be handing out some books about wood for them to search through for about ten minutes in small groups to trace the process by which trees become artefacts made of wood, such as tables. Remind them of other processes you have looked at together, for instance the journey from wheat to bread. Also remind the children of how to locate key points in a text. Tell them that it is the exact sequence of events in a process that matter – so they should perhaps look out for trigger words, such as 'first', 'begin by'; 'second' 'next' 'then'; 'lastly'. Once they have identified the main steps in the process, they might have time to note some details about each step too, such as specific terminology, tools used, different options available for the craftsmen involved.

Suggestion(s) for support
Some children may need support with cueing strategies to help them read the photocopiable sheet. An adult partner could help, or you could work with a small group of children and encourage a group reading approach.

Assessment opportunities
Note children's abiltiy to scan books for relevant information and their understanding of the importance of correct sequencing for a process. Note also their ability to interpret and follow a set of written instructions.

Opportunities for IT
Some children could experiment with different formats for showing the process, such as storyboards and flow diagrams.

Display ideas
Completed sheets and children's own suggestions for representing the process on paper could be used to make a wall display in the classroom.

Other aspects of the English PoS covered
Speaking and listening – 1a, c; 2a, b.
Writing – 1a, c; 2b, e.

Reference to photocopiable sheet
Photocopiable sheet 126 involves children in reading a jumbled set of stages in the process of turning a tree into a table. Children read the sentences, cut them out and then arrange them in the correct sequence.

When the ten minutes have passed, gather together as a class and ask the children to share their findings. Act as scribe to note on the flip chart the sequence from trees in the forest, with the help of lumberjacks making logs, to the sawmill to turn the logs into planks, to the drying rooms to season the wood ready for use, to be turned into veneers, plywood, blockwood or chipboard, to the carpenters to be shaped with a range of different tools – saws, planes, vices, drills, lathes, chisels, sandpaper, hammers – or to the builders for construction. Finally, discuss all the different ways of protecting wood by using paint, varnish, wax, polish or lacquer.

Once the children have taken on board the sequence of the process, ask the more independent learners to work individually or in pairs to devise their own way of best representing the process on paper: Would a storyboard be a good idea? Or a straightforward account in their own words? Or a flow diagram? Less experienced learners could work with photocopiable sheet 126 to re-sort the jumbled order of steps in the trees to table process. Some may need the support of an adult helper.

Suggestion(s) for extension
More confident readers could prepare a cloze task to set their peers by removing every tenth word from a text in one of the books they consulted about the process of turning trees into wooden artefacts. In a small group, their friends would decide on suitable words to fill the gaps.

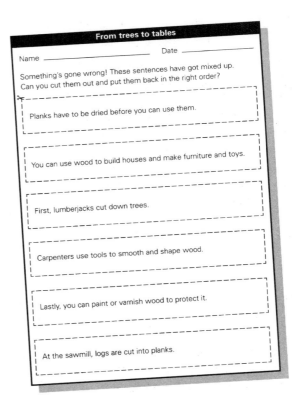

From trees to tables

Name _____ Date _____

Something's gone wrong! These sentences have got mixed up. Can you cut them out and put them back in the right order?

Planks have to be dried before you can use them.

You can use wood to build houses and make furniture and toys.

First, lumberjacks cut down trees.

Carpenters use tools to smooth and shape wood.

Lastly, you can paint or varnish wood to protect it.

At the sawmill, logs are cut into planks.

PAPER

For the children to: read and carry out a set of instructions; know that it is essential when describing a process to sequence the steps correctly; further develop research skills; read their own writing to the class.

†† **Session One**: *Oral session: whole class. Writing and paper-making sessions: small groups.* **Session Two**: *Oral session: whole class. Research session: group work. Feedback session: whole class.*

🕐 **Session One**: *Oral session: 10 minutes. Writing session: 20 minutes; paper-making slots to be arranged during the week.* **Session Two**: *Oral session: 5–10 minutes. Research session: 30–40 minutes; slots to practise writing different scripts to be arranged during the week Feedback session: 15 minutes.*

Previous skills/knowledge needed

It would be helpful if children were used to activities involving close observation and detailed oral descriptions. Some experience of reading and carrying out instructions would also be useful, as would previous experience of using writing frames to support independent research.

Key background information

Children will have come across different types of instructions in their everyday lives at home and at school, for example, recipes, instructions for assembling and making things, rules for playing games. It is wise to boost their confidence by reminding them of all of these. The key factors to point out are the relevance of the information included, the appropriate sequencing of information, specialized vocabulary and conventional formats.

The main focus of this activity is text-level work.

Preparation

Gather a collection of different sorts of paper for the children to look at carefully, feel, smell, and so on – kitchen paper, newspaper, a glossy magazine, writing paper, computer paper, wrapping paper, wallpaper, toilet paper, crêpe paper, brown paper, backing paper, Chinese art paper, confetti, doylies, cardboard plates, boxes, origami, masks, kites, blotting paper, greaseproof paper, baking paper, rice paper, tissue paper, tissues.

Copy onto a large sheet of paper the instructions for making paper, for instance from one of these reference books: *Paper* by Annabelle Dixon (A&C Black) and *Paper* by Henry Pluckrose (Watts).

Books on the history of writing will be needed in Session Two.

Resources needed

Paper-making materials and equipment (old newspapers, a clean cloth, clean absorbent paper, washing detergent, bucket, large bowl, old tablespoon, egg whisk, rolling pin, iron, mould and deckle), art and craft materials (glue, scissors, marbling inks, string, staples, paint), a flip chart, paper-making instructions, writing materials, a copy of photocopiable 127 for each child, a copy of photocopiable sheet 125 or 128 for each child (optional).

What to do

Session One

Explain to the children that you are going to look in detail at a product that comes from trees, that is, paper.

Give the children a few minutes to discuss with a partner all the different kinds of paper they can think of, together with their uses and why they are good for the job. Listen to the children's responses and bring out from an already prepared bag the wide selection of papers you collected for the session. Talk about the properties of one or two types of paper, such as the strength of brown paper that won't split for parcels, the absorbency of kitchen paper for spillages, and so on. Then divide the class into small groups to look carefully at all the different types of paper and fill in photocopiable sheet 127.

When they have finished, ask a child from each group to read their findings to the class, and comment on their lists of uses for paper.

Tell the children that, with an adult to help them over the week, they will be taking it in turns to make some paper themselves. Read to the children from the reference books about how paper is made in bulk in a factory, as well as the instructions for making paper in school. Stick the paper-making instructions, copied out onto a large sheet of paper, on the classroom wall near where the children will be working later in the week so that they can refer to them. Read them aloud together and stress how important the sequence of the steps is for any process. Tell the children to check carefully as they go through the stages of making their own paper.

Adults supervising the paper-making activity should encourage children to follow the instructions from the poster on the wall, to check that they assemble the tools and materials first, talk about the consequences of not draining the pulp well enough, of working with too much pulp at one go, of not taking care with the hot iron, of not carrying out the steps in the proper order!

Session Two

Once all the children have made paper, gather them together and tell them that the history of paper-making is linked to the history of writing. Ask what the children already know about early forms of writing – perhaps some of them might have visited caves in other countries and seen early cave paintings, some may have heard of the Rosetta stone, some may have visited the British Museum or even been to Egypt. *How did people pass on their stories and their life histories before writing was invented?* See if they know what utensils people have used to make marks with, in the past as well as the present, or if they know whether everybody in the community was always taught to write. Do they know how books are produced today?

When all the children's ideas have been aired, scribe onto the flip chart, in the form of a set of questions, what the children still want to find out. Divide the children into groups according to interest, and set them the task of finding the answers to the questions. You could offer a writing frame to support their research (see photocopiable sheets 125 and 128). As always, share the finished work and reflect on what has been learned, by referring back to the original set of questions on the flip chart.

As a follow-up activity, you might like to arrange a visit to a museum to look at old books; books on vellum, parchment, papyrus, silk and so on, and manuscripts with beautiful illuminations; clay tablets; cuneiform writing; hieroglyphs; Cyrillic, Hebrew and Arabic scripts and Chinese characters.

You could also set up sessions for the children to experiment with writing other scripts, such as Chinese, Urdu or Russian. Involve people from the local community if possible to demonstrate their writing system.

Suggestion(s) for extension
Independent readers and writers could put their research findings to good use by writing non-fiction books.

Suggestion(s) for support
Some children will benefit from the support of an adult or more able peer to help them read and follow the instructions for making paper. You could supply children with key-word scanning cards to help them locate information for their research work.

Assessment opportunities
Note the children's use of descriptive vocabulary when discussing the qualities of the various types of paper; the range of cueing strategies they use to read the set of instructions; their growing competence in research skills when exploring the history of writing; their confidence in presenting their findings to the class when reporting back.

Opportunities for IT
Bilingual children could experiment with software that uses scripts other than the Roman alphabet.

Display ideas
There are ample opportunities here for display: the children's home-made paper, their accounts of the paper-making session, comparisons between the properties of different types of paper, research notes and 'published' non-fiction books.

Other aspects of English PoS covered
Speaking and listening – 1a, c, d; 2a, b; 3b.
Writing – 1a, b, c; 2a, b, c, d, e; 3a.

Reference to photocopiable sheets

Photocopiable sheet 127 involves children in noting the main properties of different types of paper and listing possible uses.

Photocopiable sheets 125 and 128 can be offered as sample writing frames to support children's research in this activity.

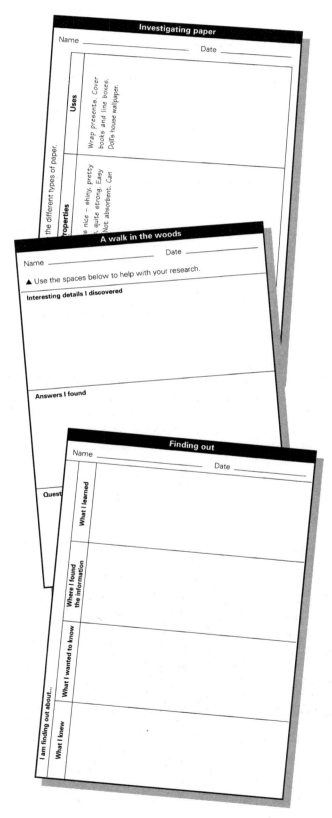

FIRE

For the children to: make explicit what they already know about a specific topic, and generate questions about what they need to find out; use structural guides to scan texts and find relevant information quickly; recognize that non-fiction books on similar themes can give different information and present similar information in different ways; compare information from a range of sources.

†† *Introductory oral session: whole class. Research/ writing sessions: children working in groups. Feedback session: whole class. Writing/drawing session(s): children working individually.*

🕐 *Introductory oral session: 25 minutes. Research/ writing sessions: 25 minutes each. Feedback session: 30 minutes. Writing/drawing session(s): 20–25 minutes.*

Previous skills/knowledge needed

It would be helpful if the children had some experience of identifying what they know and what they want to know about a topic. It would also help if they had experience of scanning texts and were accustomed to being critically aware and to evaluating what they read from different sources.

Key background information

Children should be taught to consider every possible source of information when researching a topic – books, both non-fiction and fiction, plays, songs, letters, newspapers and magazines, archive documents, photographs, films, television programmes and videos, oral histories and eye-witness accounts, objects, museum displays, buildings, and so on.

Teachers should encourage them to develop a sense of sequence, of chronology, and help them to compare differences between ways of life at different times, and to understand the impact on people's lives of historical changes. They need to grow increasingly aware of the need to evaluate the accuracy of information texts and not just accept as gospel everything in print!

Preparation

Gather a collection of books and articles connected with the topic of fire; bundles of firewood, logs, pieces of coal, charcoal, anthracite; artefacts, such as tapers, camping stoves, firelighters; photographs of homes in times past. Also check with your local Schools Library Service regarding the availability of videos on the topic.

Resources needed

Books about fire, tape recorders and cassettes, notebooks, drawing materials (including charcoal), writing materials, a flip chart, a copy of photocopiable sheet 128 for each child, a copy of photocopiable sheet 125 for each child (optional).

What to do

Ask the children how their houses are heated – gas fires, electric fires, central heating with gas, electricity, oil? Remind the children that one of the properties of wood is that it will burn. Check to see if any of them have an open fire in their house. If so, what do they burn – coal, charcoal, anthracite, logs? Who is responsible for seeing to the fire? How often do they light it? What work is involved in lighting it and keeping the grate clean? How often is the chimney swept? Who does that? What do they especially like/dislike about having an open fire in their home? Find out if any of the children have ever been camping and discuss what they used then to keep warm and to cook their food.

Move on to discuss what they use at home to cook their meals: gas, electric, Aga, microwave oven? How many of them have barbecues in the summer? What do they think are the advantages and disadvantages of the various methods? See if they also know how their water is heated at home for washing and so on. Brainstorm all the choices people have today with regard to heating and cooking and write these on the flip chart. Also make a note of any key words that might support the children's research later.

Now, ask the children to think about the options that people had in the past, for instance how did their grandparents keep warm and cook food? Note their ideas,

then suggest that they need to find out more. Consider the sources available to them:

▲ Interview some older people in their family or in the local community about what it was like in their home when they were little.
▲ Look at videos and/or television programmes.
▲ Check books, old documents, archive material of the local newspaper.
▲ Visit a museum.
▲ Look at old photographs.

Divide the class into groups to investigate as many of these as possible, making each group responsible for gathering the information from one particular source. Interviews can be conducted at home or in school, depending on the interviewees.

Before they begin their research hunt, discuss significant factors to bear in mind, such as *why* changes were made – cost, convenience, pollution, supply, technological advances. Each method of heating and cooking is bound to have some pros and cons! They might also like to bear in mind aspects such as social class differences and gender differences. Finally, remind the class about the steps to take when carrying out information-seeking research: what they know – want to know – new information learned – evaluation. Hand out photocopiable sheet 128 and read the headings with the class before they begin their task.

When the groups have concluded their tasks, come together as a whole class to report back to each other and to compare findings. Any discrepancies between sources

should be discussed and reasons sought. You could talk about:

▲ technical vocabulary and the use or lack of glossary

▲ the visual support in texts – photographs versus illustrations

▲ the usefulness of diagrams and charts

▲ the support of captions, headings, sub-headings, layout

▲ the date of publication

▲ the author's qualifications

▲ whether it has full or missing facts

▲ its lack or surfeit of detail

▲ any one-sided views or opinions presented as facts

▲ people's faulty memories

▲ visual and spoken material versus written (photographers and directors can also be biased).

Time will need to be allocated for the children to write and draw, in order to mount a display about all that they have found out between them.

Suggestion(s) for extension

Independent learners might like to investigate another strand and explore prehistoric peoples and the discovery of fire, and the transformations it brought to their lives in terms of warmth, light and cooking possibilities. They could also investigate fire in its role as a warning symbol, for example on beacons in the Napoleonic Wars. In each case remind them to be critically alert when consulting their sources.

Suggestion(s) for support

It is easier to read for information if you are familiar with the topic and know some of the specialized vocabulary. Thus it is specially important for less experienced readers to be introduced to key vocabulary in the introductory session.

For the research session, it is essential to provide books at the right reading level for these children, with some pictorial support and less dense text. Avoid giving them newspaper articles and archive materials or pamphlets that can be difficult to access.

Assessment opportunities

Children's skills at formulating questions for research and locating and retrieving information can be monitored. Note also their growing understanding about the range of sources available, the need to compare and contrast and to evaluate findings. Their developing writing and presentation skills will be apparent in the work they produce for the classroom display.

Opportunities for IT

All the writing for the display could be produced using IT. Children could also make games for their peers using their own pieces of writing – cloze procedure, text completion and '20 questions' quiz games.

Display ideas

Children could mount a display of the project showing their lists of sources, a comparison of various sources, the results of their research, comments about what they enjoyed most, what surprised them most and so on. Paintings, drawings, artefacts, photos, videos, taped interviews and books would enhance the overall effect.

Other aspects of English PoS covered

Speaking and listening – 1a, c, d; 2a, b; 3a.
Writing – 1 a, c; 2b, c, d, e; 3a.

Reference to photocopiable sheets

Photocopiable sheet 128 provides an extended framework to help children establish good habits of research.

Photocopiable sheet 125 can also be offered as a research support tool.

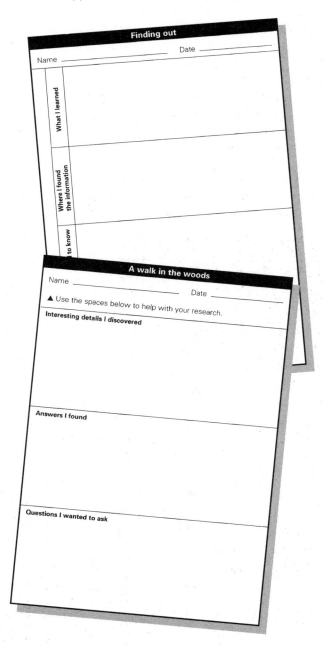

Signs and symbols

Name _____ Date _____

▲ Look carefully at the scene below. Cut out the notices and stick
each one in the proper place on the picture, over the correct symbol.

		No parking	Parking
No smoking	Bus stop	No right turn	No left turn
Hospital	Toilets	No dogs	Cycle lane

Weather reports

Name _____ Date _____

▲ Look carefully at this map of Britain. Fill in the missing words for the weather report that goes with it.

Friday's weather

A _____ and _____ day with _____ spreading slowly across the country.

In southern England it will be _____ _____.

In the _____ there will be outbreaks of _____, and winds will be _____ mph.

In Scotland it will be _____ with _____ all day and strong winds near _____ force.

Ireland will have blustery _____ with some _____. Later, strong _____ will blow from the west.

Shops: What's in a name?, see page 17

Shops

Name _____   Date _____

▲ Read the shop names below and put a ring around the odd one out in each row. Then give your reason.

1 McDonald's, Mothercare, Wimpy, Burger King

Why? _____

2 Boots, TopShop, Burton, Etam

Why? _____

3 British Home Stores, Littlewoods, Woolworths, Dolcis

Why? _____

4 Asda, Tesco, Iceland, Safeway

Why? _____

5 Toys Я Us, Currys, Southern Electric, Dixons

Why? _____

6 Our Price, Barclays, HMV, Virgin

Why? _____

▲ Now make up some more for your friends to do:

Doing the shopping, see page 19

Supermarkets

These notices have got all mixed up. Cut them out and stick them in three groups in the right place in the table provided.

Apples	Parking	Cakes	Pears
Ice Cream	Petrol	Chips	Staff Only
Entrance	Meat	Biscuits	Exit
Oranges	Mangoes	Disabled Parking	Grapefruit
Fire	Rice	Figs	Bread
Pasta	Rhubarb	Sauces	Plums
Grapes	Recycling	Tea	Raspberries
Exit	Bananas	Coffee	Cereals
Cheese	Pet Food	Fish	Pineapples
Lemons	Strawberries	Emergency Exit	Toilets

Doing the shopping, see page 19

Supermarkets (cont.)

Name _____ Date _____

Signs you'd see outside a supermarket	Notices for the main shopping aisles	Labels for the fruit section

Breakfast cereals, see page 21

Cereals

Name _____   Date _____

▲ Think of a name for a new cereal then design a packet for it.

My poster to promote sales would say:

Who's talking?, see page 30

Gossip

Name _____ Date _____

▲ Write in the speech bubbles what you think the elephants might be saying to one another.

Who's talking?

Name _____ Date _____

▲ Write out in sentences in the spaces below what the elephants Elmer, Wilbur, Arthur, Martha and Lucy were saying. Don't forget the speech marks!

You could use some of the words provided in the box.

said	asked
whispered	begged
shouted	laughed
cried	muttered

1 _____

_____

2 _____

_____

3 _____

_____

4 _____

_____

5 _____

_____

Opposites, see page 36

Find the opposites!

Name _____ Date _____

▲ Choose from this box of words the ones that best describe the
opposite of the weather conditions listed below. Then write your
choices in the empty column.

dry	dull	cloudy	chilly	windy
hot	misty	scorching	foggy	raining

bright	
sunny	
wet	
mild	
calm	
clear	
freezing	
fine	

Opposites, see page 36

What's the weather like?

Name _____   Date _____

▲ Read carefully, then finish
the sentences below in as
interesting a way as you can.

The weather was as wet as _____

_____

It was as calm as _____

_____

It is as clear as _____

_____

The sun was as bright as _____

_____

The day was as dull as _____

_____

It felt as cold as _____

_____

The air is as hot as _____

_____

The sky was as dark as _____

_____

Narrative structure, see page 39

Storyboard

Name _____ Date _____

▲ Draw and write about the main events in your chosen story.

The beginning	The middle	The end

Narrative structure, see page 39

Story outline

Name ______________________ Date ______________

▲ Complete the outline of your chosen story in the spaces below.

The beginning (Where? When? Who?)

The story takes place

____

The main characters are

____

The middle (What are the main events?)

One day ____

____

Then ____

____

At last ____

____

The end (What happens?)

So, they _______________________________________

____

____

Short story genre, see page 41

Novels v short stories

Name _____   Date _____

▲ Read the statements carefully, then put a tick in the column you think each one applies to.

Comments	Novels	Short stories
The story has a beginning, middle and end.		
There is a list of contents.		
There is a list of chapters.		
You can read it in any order.		
You don't have to read the whole book.		
It is easy to read on your own.		
You get a variety of stories in one book.		
I can write stories like this.		
You can get a variety of authors in one book.		
It is exciting to look forward to the next chapter.		
The writer can take more time to set the scene.		
There's more space for details.		
You have time to get to know the characters well.		
The tension builds up as the story develops.		

I like to read _____

because _____

_____

Listen and learn, see page 43

A parade! A parade!

A parade! A parade!
A rum-a-te-tum
I know a parade
By the sound of the drum
A rum-a-te-tum
A rum-a-te-tum
A rum-a-te-tum-a-te-tum.

Here it comes, down the street
A rum-a-te-tum
I know a parade
By the sound of the feet
A rum-a-te-tum
A rum-a-te-tum
A rum-a-te-tum-a-te-tum.

Music and feet, music and feet
A rum-a-te-tum
Can't you feel
The sound of the beat?
A rum-a-te-tum.
A rum-a-te-tum
A rum-a-te-tum-a-te-tum.

Listen and learn, see page 43

My parade poem

Name _____ Date _____

▲ Fill in the spaces to make your own poem about the sounds of a parade.

A parade! A parade!

A rum-a-te-tum

I know a parade

_____

A rum-a-te-tum

A rum-a-te-tum

A rum-a-te-tum-a-te-tum.

Here it comes, down the street

A rum-a-te-tum

I know a parade

_____

A rum-a-te-tum

A rum-a-te-tum

A rum-a-te-tum-a-te-tum.

_____

A rum-a-te-tum

Can't you feel

_____ ?

A rum-a-te-tum

A rum-a-te-tum

A rum-a-te-tum-a-te-tum.

Hippopotamus dancing

In the hippo house
at the city zoo,
hippos are moving
to the boogaloo,
big hippos shuffle,
little hippos trot,
everyone giving it
all they've got.

Hip-hippo, hippopotamus dancing,
Hip-hippo, hippopotamus dancing.

Every hippo
keeping fit,
fighting the flab,
doing their bit,
weight-training one week,
aerobics another,
tiny hippopotami
move with their mothers.

Keep listening and learning, see page 45

Hippopotamus dancing (cont.)

Hip-hippo, hippopotamus dancing,
Hip-hippo, hippopotamus dancing.

Hippos in tutus,
hippos in vests,
baby hippos
doing their best
to keep clear of Dad
as he stumbles around,
causing commotion,
shaking the ground.

Hip-hippo, hippopotamus dancing,
Hip-hippo, hippopotamus dancing.

Brian Moses

Listen, learn and think!, see page 47

Trouble at the Dinosaur Café

Down at the Dinosaur Café
everybody was doing fine.
Steggy was slurping his swamp juice
while Iggy sat down to dine.

Bronto was eating his tree roots
and had ordered vegetable pie,
when in stomped Tyrannosaurus
with a wicked gleam in his eye.

He read the menu from left to right
then gobbled it up in one gulp.
He chewed upon it thoughtfully
as the paper turned to pulp.

"You plant eaters are fine," he said,
"if that's all you want to eat,
but I'm a growing dinosaur
and my stomach cries out for meat.

Listen, learn and think!, see page 47

Trouble at the Dinosaur Café (cont.)

"I need something extra
to get me through my day.
I do lots of ROARING and BELLOWING,
I just can't get by on hay."

Steggy stiffened, Iggy trembled,
while Bronto fell off his chair.
Tyrannosaurus turned his head
and fixed them with his stare:

"There's nothing I like more," he said,
"than a tasty dinosaur stew,
and for extra special flavour
I'll add YOU
        and YOU
        and YOU!"

Brian Moses

Listen, learn and think!, see page 47

Find a rhyme

Name _____   Date _____

▲ Collect as many words as you can that rhyme with the words below.

pie	eat	stew

▲ Look carefully. Do the words always **look** alike as well as **sound** alike?

Creating a class anthology, see page 49

My favourite poem

Name _____ Date _____

Poem:_____

I like this poem because _____

_____

_____

_____

My favourite part is _____

_____

_____

Here are the words/phrases that I like best:_____

_____

_____

_____

I know some other poems by the same writer:_____

_____

I know some other poems on the same theme:_____

_____

All join in!, see page 53

How many syllables?

Name _____ Date _____

▲ Hunt for words with the same number of syllables as the words below. Add any more of your own that you think of.

chips (1)	chicken (2)	everyone (3)

Can you find any words with 4 syllables?

Visiting poet, see page 55

Display plan

Name _____   Date _____

Decide which items you want to put in each space.
Don't forget the headings!

Anything they can do…, see page 57

Monday's child is red and spotty

Monday's child is red and spotty,

Tuesday's child won't use the potty.

Wednesday's child won't go to bed.

Thursday's child will not be fed.

Friday's child breaks all his toys,

Saturday's child makes an awful noise.

And the child that's born on the seventh day

Is a pain in the neck like the rest, OK!

Colin McNaughton

Anything they can do..., see page 57

Monday's child is...

Name ______________________ Date ______________

Here is your chance to create a new poem.

▲ Share some ideas with a friend before you write.

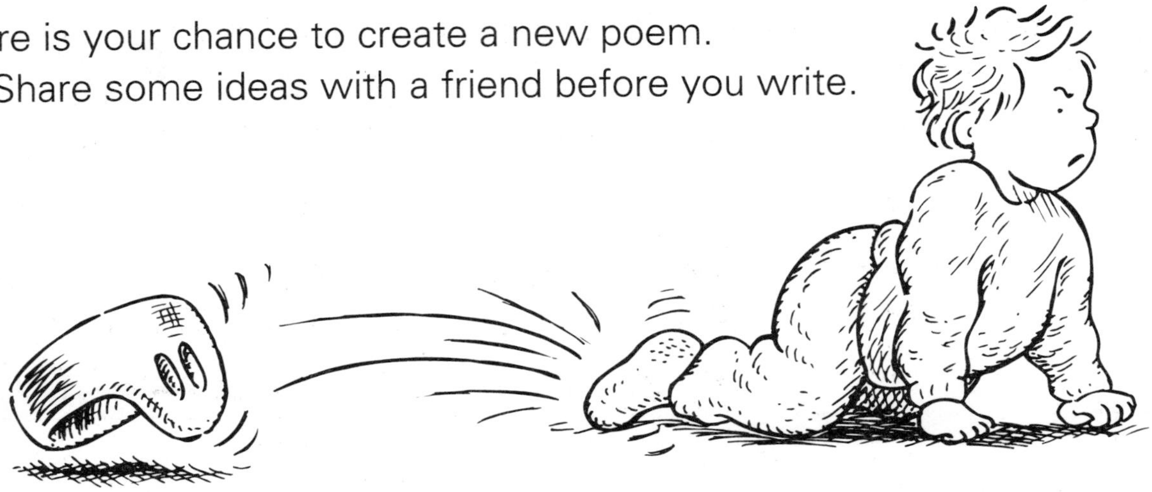

Monday's child is ______________________

Tuesday's child is ______________________

Wednesday's child is ______________________

Thursday's child is ______________________

Friday's child is ______________________

Saturday's child is ______________________

But the child that is born on the Sabbath day

Is ______________________.

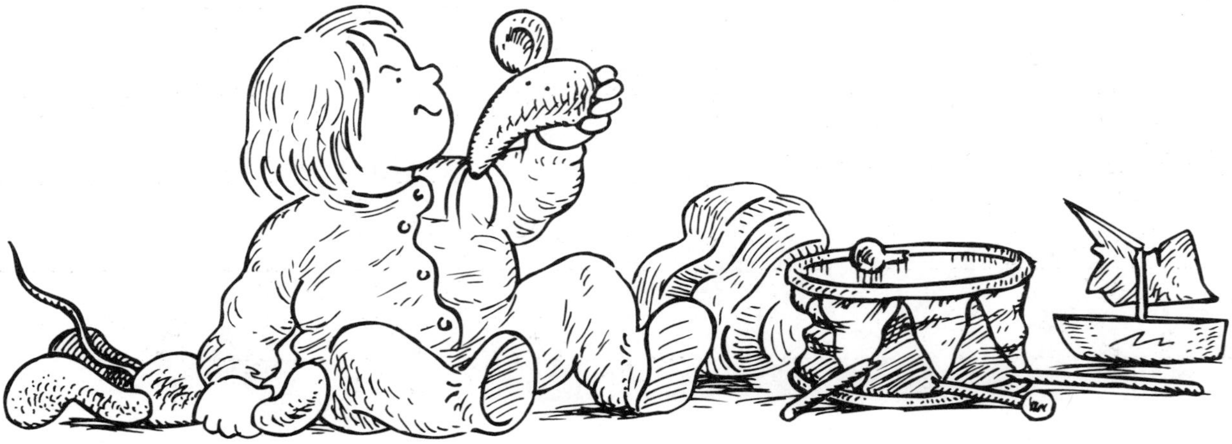

Illnesses and accidents, see page 75

In the kitchen

Name _____ Date _____

▲ Look carefully at this picture of a kitchen. Put a circle around all the things that you think are wrong and that might cause an accident.
▲ On the back of this sheet, write down how they could be made safe.

A healthy diet, see page 77

What I have eaten

Name _____ Date _____

▲ Write down everything you eat this week and put a tick in the appropriate column to show its value.

Food	Protein	Vitamins	Carbohydrate	Fibre	Fat
Monday					
Tuesday					
Thursday					
Friday					
Saturday					
Sunday					

A walk in the woods, see page 85; Paper, see page 89 and Fire, see page 91

A walk in the woods

Name _____ Date _____

▲ Use the spaces below to help with your research.

Interesting details I discovered

Answers I found

Questions I wanted to ask

From trees to tables, see page 87

From trees to tables

Name _____ Date _____

Something's gone wrong! These sentences have got mixed up.
Can you cut them out and put them back in the right order?

Planks have to be dried before you can use them.

You can use wood to build houses and make furniture and toys.

First, lumberjacks cut down trees.

Carpenters use tools to smooth and shape wood.

Lastly, you can paint or varnish wood to protect it.

At the sawmill, logs are cut into planks.

Paper, see page 89

Investigating paper

Name _____ Date _____

▲ Fill in the columns to best describe the different types of paper.

Type of paper	Properties	Uses
Wrapping paper	Feels nice. Looks nice – shiny, pretty pattern. Smooth, quite strong. Easy to cut and fold. Not absorbent. Can roll it.	Wrap presents. Cover books and line boxes. Doll's house wallpaper.

Paper, see page 89 and Fire, see page 91

Finding out

Name _____   Date _____

I am finding out about...	What I knew	What I wanted to know	Where I found the information	What I learned